FOR MY BUDDY CHESTER

From mangy street dog to expert motorcycle rider you're the best traveling companion a guy could have.

Thank you for barking at all the cows, horses, cars, bicycles and birds.

Looking forward to more great adventures with you

Contents

08
Colombia Is The Perfect Place To Start In South America

Introduction	6
Colombia Is The Perfect Place To Start In South America	8
Is Colombia Safe?	**13**
The Only Risk Is Wanting To Stay	13
No Dar Papaya	14
The Geography of Colombia	**15**
Triple Andes	15
Colombia: An Off-Road Riders Paradise	16
Limited Highway Construction	16
Isolated Communities	16
Fourth Generation (4G) Road Program	16
Renting	**18**
Good For Short Term Travel	18
Low Cost	18
Less Hassle	18
Motorcycle Tours	**19**
Independent vs. guided	19
Independent	19
Guided Tours	20
What's the best type of motorcycle to ride in Colombia?	**19**
Small, Light and Nimble	23
Suzuki DR650	25
Honda Tornado 250	28
Satellite GPS Tracker	**29**
Buying & Selling A Motorcycle In Colombia	**30**
Can I import a motorcycle to Colombia then sell it?	30
Can I buy a motorcycle in Colombia then sell it in another country?	30
Why are vehicles so expensive in Colombia?	30
How To Buy A Motorcycle In Colombia	**31**
Registering with the RUNT	31
Find a Motorcycle	32
Mechanical Inspection	32
Check all documents - The most important part!	32
Transferring ownership	35
Paying	36
Shipping A Motorcycle	**37**
The Darién Gap	37
What is the Darién Gap?	37
Why is it difficult to cross?	37
Why isn't there a road?	38
Has Anyone Ever Been Able To Cross The Darién?	38
How to Ship Your Bike Across the Darién Gap	**39**
How to fly your bike across the Darién Gap	40
How to share a shipping container with other vehicles	40
How to RORO your bike across the Darién Gap	41
Town To Town	42
Driving in Colombia	**43**
Required Documents	44
Licencia - Driver's License	44
Matrícula – Registration papers	44
SOAT – Third Party Insurance	44
Técnico Mecánica	44
Required gear	44
Emergency Tool Kit	44
Recommended Gear	45
Buying a SIM Card	47
Driving Conditions in Colombia	**48**
General Chaos & Mayhem	50
Lane splitting	50

JEFF & ALAN'S GUIDE TO MOTORCYCLE TRAVEL IN COLOMBIA

23
What's the best type of motorcycle to ride in Colombia?
Small, Light and Nimble	23
Suzuki DR650	25
Honda Tornado 250	28

Hidden Colombian Speed Bumps	50
Elusive Road Signs	50
Hitchhiking Cyclists	51
Gravity Bikes	51
Painted Lines	51
Livestock	51
No Headlights	51
Wrong-Way	51
Families Walking In Blind Curves	51
Sinkholes	51
Parking Anywhere	51
The Biggest Danger: You	52
Local Knowledge	**53**
Speed Limits & Speed Cameras in Colombia	54
Speed Cameras	54
Highway Tolls	55
Pico y Placa	55
Motorcycle Parking	55
Getting Gas	55
What to Do if You're Stopped by the Police	56

Emergency 123	57
Repair Shops	57
Planning Your Own Route	**58**
When is the best time to visit Colombia?	58
Planning Your Own Route	60
Google Street View	60
iOverlander	60
Motorcycle Navigation in Colombia	60
Google Maps	60
Gaia GPS	61
Paper Maps	61
Accommodation	61
Hotels	61
Camping	62
Where to Camp	62
How Much Does It Cost To Travel In Colombia?	**63**
Bueno, Bonito, Barato	63
Itineraries	**66**
Medellín - A Starting Point	66
Airport	66
Weather	67
Things to Do	69
About Our Itineraries	72
Day Trips From Medellín	**73**
The Milk Route	74
Guatapé	78
Cocorná	80
Overnight Trips	**86**
San Carlos	88
Jardin	92
Jerico	94
One Week Trips	**96**
Windows of Tisquizoque	98
The Perfect Loop:	102
Exploring The Coffee Region	102
Journey To The Jungle	114
More Than A Week	**120**
Medellín- Cartagena Loop	134
Exploring The Eastern Mountain Ranges	145
Caño Cristales	155
Where Not To Go	**156**
The Worst Road in Colombia	156
Bogotá	157
Salento	157
Jeff Cremer	
Interview	**160**
Alan Churchill Interview	**164**
Conclusion	167
Image Credits:	167

JEFF & ALAN'S GUIDE TO MOTORCYCLE TRAVEL IN COLOMBIA

Introduction

The world we know is a place filled with coffee shops, strip malls, and social media. In the heart of the Colombian Andes, the veneer of "civilization" is stripped away and true adventure can still be found. From towering, snow-covered volcanoes and misty jungle mountains to remote rivers and quaint coffee farming villages: Colombia is a land of extremes. You've probably been dreaming about a trip like this but have had some doubts. We aim to give you the confidence and know-how so that you can do it on your own and be successful. We want to remove any uncertainties before you take the plunge and throw yourself into a new culture and discover motorcycling outside your borders. Considering how easy it is for people to travel around Colombia, it's surprising that many people decide to stay "safe" (and bored) back in their hometown.

Colombia is actually a totally safe place. In fact, 4.5 million people decided to make the

jump and travel to Colombia in 2019. Despite this, many people still see a motorcycle trip to Colombia as something that's simply out of the question. Unknown factors such as cost and safety can hold some people back. For others, the uncertainty of where to stay, where to go, and who to rent a motorcycle from can also be barriers. Sadly, all these factors together prevent people from motorcycling one of the most beautiful and friendly countries in the world.

Scattered throughout message boards and hidden in small Facebook groups lay bits and pieces of information from previous travelers who were simply passing through. Information can be outdated, incorrect, and unorganized. Sifting through all this information can be challenging and time-consuming. What you want is to create a clear mental picture of riding conditions in the country; what you need is accurate information all in one place. This book is going to give you that.

After working as a wildlife photographer in the Peruvian Amazon, I decided to take the leap and move to Colombia. For the past three years, I've owned and operated www.ColombiaMotoAdventures.com a full-service motorcycle rental and tour agency based in Medellín. Starting from nothing, I had to work to buy motorcycles, put together compelling itineraries, find quality hotels, and do a million other tasks that make a travel business successful.

Based on my personal experiences, as well as the experiences of hundreds of satisfied customers, I've compiled as much information as possible and put it all into one place. Even better, it's all up to date. Standard details on accommodation, recommended motorcycles and gear is included. More specific information about how to buy a motorcycle and cross the Darrien Gap can also be found inside. Travel tips about filling up on gas, getting through toll booths, and purchasing a cell phone SIM card are also included – all this will have you riding like a local in no time.

Jerico, Colombia

> Based on my personal experiences of hundreds of satisfied customers, I've compiled as much information as possible and put it all into one place.

Riding a motorcycle is the best way to experience a foreign country. A friend of mine once mentioned that once you cross the border and get into South America, your senses go on overload. From smelling the smoke while riding past burning sugar cane fields, to feeling the cool perfumed jungle air at night, not to mention taking in spectacular vistas around almost every turn, a trip through Colombia is an experience that's impossible to forget.

When talking about adventure and travel, whether it's with an old friend or a stranger, it seems like everyone has a desire to explore new places and see the world. If you've been wanting to go on an adventurous, exciting motorcycle trip but had some doubts, just read this guide and don't let anything hold you back.

The only risk is wanting to stay.

Jeff Cremer

Colombia Is The Perfect Place To Start In South America

El Peñol de Guatapé is a landmark of Antioquia

↑ The rural town of Belmira, Colombia

Ready to take a motorcycle ride through South America? Colombia, nicknamed "The Gateway to South America", is the perfect place to start! Allow me to opine...

COLOMBIA HAS THE BEST OF EVERYTHING

There is a saying that goes "If you want the best Caribbean beaches to go to the Bahamas, if you want the best Amazon go to Peru, if you want the most amazing Andes go to Brazil, but if you want them all in one place, go to Colombia. If you're short on time, you can experience a little bit of everything that makes South America magical. Rather than rush through a whole continent in 2-3 months, barely seeing anything except asphalt and gas stations, choose one spot and see it well.

UNEXPLORED AND UNDISCOVERED...

Colombia is a country that not even the locals have thoroughly explored. With the improved political situation, huge areas that were formerly off-limits to tourists are now open for business – locals and foreigners alike are finally exploring their own fantastic backyard. It wasn't that long ago that places like the Lost City in Santa Marta or Comuna 13 in Medellín were totally off-limits and, nowadays, they're becoming downright tourist hubs.

...BUT NOT FOR LONG

We recommend coming to Colombia sooner rather than later. Colombia still feels new and authentic and it's worth getting here first before it too gets overrun by mass tourism.

↑ Guatapé makes a great day trip and is located only 1-1/2 hours from Medellín

IT'S THE MOST OBVIOUS 'BREAK' ON A PAN-AMERICAN MOTORCYCLE TOUR

Not everyone has the chance to traverse two continents in one trip. Most of the time, adventure riders will actually split up North and South America into two journeys, taken even a few years apart. Colombia is the most obvious place to break up the long-haul odyssey in two and is absolutely genius for North American riders, who can explore their continent on their own bike and then fly to Colombia (either shipping their bike or buying one here) and continuing south to Ushuaia.

↑ The rugged landscape of the Colombian coffee region

My friend Phil showing the beautiful mountains outside of Medellín

YOU CAN SKIP THE DRAMA OF THE DARIÉN

Shipping your bike is expensive, time-consuming, and nerve-wracking at the best of times. Unless you're on a bucket list trip that specifically includes a trip through Central America, you can skip the drama of the Darién and start your trip in Medellín. You'll still have the best of South America at your feet.

PERFECT CLIMATE YEAR-ROUND

The equatorial climate means you can start your South America adventure trip at any time of year, even winter, and travel south as spring and summer hit. Colombia allows you more flexibility in travel which is pivotal for a motorcycle trip.

FRIENDLY PEOPLE

We find Colombians to be among the friendliest people in all of Latin America and they're a huge reason we call this place home. Locals are not just interested in meeting foreigners but they're incessantly eager to help out. No matter what issue you may be facing on your travels, don't be shy: if you've lost your way or need some assistance on the road, chances are you'll find it at a moment's notice if you simply ask.

LOCATION

Medellín is surprisingly close to the United States and is only a 3.5-hour direct flight from Miami. Another good thing is that since Colombia is directly south of the United States, the time zones won't change that much, if at all, which helps you avoid jet lag. Also, when it's winter in the states, it's summer in Colombia which means that Colombia is the perfect place to visit if you want to escape the winter and ride.

CHILL OUT AND LEARN SOME SPANISH

Colombia is an insanely popular place to take Spanish language classes and here you'll find some of the best language schools in South America! Add to this the fantastic weather and friendly locals and it's easy to see why "hanging around" for a while, before tackling a full continental crossing, is an excellent idea. Chilling out in Colombia will also help you get a feel for the culture, let you get into the flow of the trip as well as get any of the bugs worked out before you head off on your journey.

Is Colombia Safe?

THE ONLY RISK IS WANTING TO STAY

The number one question we are asked regarding travel in Colombia is "Is it safe?" For many years it wasn't. When people think of Colombia, the legacy of drug cartels, Pablo Escobar, and the FARC guerrillas are what people first talk about. The reality is that Colombia is now one of the safest countries in Latin America.

The reduction in crime and a peace deal to end a 50-year conflict with the FARC communist rebels has encouraged a remarkable spike in tourism. In 2019, the country welcomed a record-breaking tourist crowd of over 4.5 million visitors. This has led to the construction of new international airports as well as major airlines flocking to add Colombia to their list of destinations.

The city of Medellín, Colombia, is often considered a success story and an international benchmark for urban transformation and social innovation. Once considered the "Murder Capital of the World", Medellín had very high levels of poverty, inequality, and social exclusion. However, in only two decades, the city has managed to transform itself into a safer, more inclusive, and prosperous place that has

> *If you want the best Caribbean beaches to go to the Bahamas, if you want the best Amazon go to Peru, if you want the most amazing Andes go to Peru, but if you want them all in one place, go to Colombia.*

Medellín is surrounded by mountains and it is very clean with lush trees and beautiful flowers

> *If you want to find bad people in Colombia, you can surely find them, as you could in New York or Los Angeles.* **But nowhere have my crew and I been treated better or with more kindness and generosity.** *I'd bring my family on vacation there in a heartbeat. And hope to soon. As I said before: Colombians are proud. Let them show you what they are proud of."*
>
> ANTHONY BOURDAIN

↑ Even police checkpoints are friendly

received attention and recognition, recently being named "The World's Most Innovative City" by the Wall Street Journal. Colombia has fought hard to rid itself of crime and violence and has now re-emerged as one of the most exhilarating travel destinations in the world

So pack your bags and let's go ride!

NO DAR PAPAYA

No dar papaya literally means to 'not give papaya' but it has nothing to do with fruit – this actually means "don't put yourself in a position where people can easily take advantage of you."

No dar papaya when traveling means don't walk around with an expensive camera around your neck and a guide-book in your hand, don't leave your cell phone on tables, walk dodgy city areas at night or go home with someone you've just met in a club. Needless to say, keep away from drugs of any kind and from anyone who deals in drugs. Because if you go looking for trouble, in Colombia, or anywhere for that matter, trust that it will find you.

Stay alert, keep your wits about you, be on the lookout for potential trouble…and you can be sure you won't be giving any papaya.

The Geography of Colombia

Why is motorcycle travel so great in Colombia? To sum it up, three high altitude mountain ranges and impassable jungles have made creating transportation infrastructure a monumentally difficult task. With only winding unpaved dirt roads to connect areas of the country, many small towns and villages are still largely isolated from the major cities of the country. While this makes transporting cargo and general transportation difficult, the rough terrain makes Colombia seem like it was tailor-made for ADV motorcycle touring.

Let's go into more detail:

TRIPLE ANDES

Colombia has some incredible geography due to its unique position in the world. Sitting on top of a rare and complex junction of three tectonic plates (Nazca, Caribbean, and South American plates) Colombia has been in the middle of a huge geological head-on collision for the past 50 million years.

When these tectonic plates collided they created something called a subduction zone. These subduction zones happen when one plate sinks into the mantle underneath the other plate. The pressure from the tectonic plate diving down forced magma to squirt up towards the surface creating the huge Andes mountain range as well as creating a chain of volcanoes.

As you know, Colombia is located in the Andes mountain range. What you may not know is that the Andes range actually splits into three in Colombia like a three-pronged fork with valleys between each mountain range. These three mountain ranges, called "Cordilleras", consist of the:

- Cordillera Occidental (Western Range)

↑ Rugged mountainous landscape of Colombia

- Cordillera Central (Central Range)
- Cordillera Oriental (Eastern Range)

Combined, these cordilleras are three times the length of the Alps. The Colombian Andes are also higher than the Alps, with the tallest mountain in Colombia topping out at a staggering 5,775 masl. Mont Blanc, standing at 4,810 masl, would only be the 8th tallest mountain if it were in Colombia. Compared to the Rocky Mountains in the United States, the tallest mountain is only 4,401 masl and wouldn't even make the list of Colombia's top 10 tallest mountains. When the low-lying valleys sit at a height of 8,000 feet / 2,700 meters, you understand just how colossal these mountains are.

Colombia: An Off-Road Riders Paradise

Colombia's rough geography and mountainous terrain is bad news for day-to-day transit but great news for adventure riders!

LIMITED HIGHWAY CONSTRUCTION

As we mentioned earlier, Colombia is split by the Andes into three chains of mountains, and, what's more, its entire Pacific coast is completely obstructed by impenetrable jungle. These geographical characteristics make it a formidable task to build transport infrastructure: the average cost of building a road in the Colombian Andes is an insane $10 million USD per kilometer, which is significantly higher than in the US (USD 2.25 million) or Europe (USD 2.6 million).

For this reason, it's not surprising to learn that only 15% of Colombia's roads are paved. Even more incredible, the country has just 1,000 kilometers of dual-lane divided highways -the remainder of the transportation network is made up of over 150,000km of unpaved roads. You could spend your entire life riding the dirt roads here and hardly ever find the need to touch tarmac!

Another interesting fact is that this lack of infrastructure has led to Colombia having the second-lowest vehicle ownership rate in all of South America and outside of major cities, you can count on seeing very little traffic.

ISOLATED COMMUNITIES

This lack of transportation infrastructure has made it hard to connect isolated communities. Outside of the three major populated areas of Medellín, Cali, and Bogotá, the mountainous Andes and vast jungles remain largely uninhabited with spots of civilization scattered throughout the country. Nestled deep within the rugged terrain, some of these villages are perched in seemingly impossible-to-reach locations. Although it takes a little work to get there, when you finally arrive, these towns look like they've been plucked from a fairytale book; seemingly untouched by the passing of time. Exploring these places is an unforgettable experience, but you'll need to hurry up and visit. Due to the expansion of the road network these towns won't stay isolated for long.

FOURTH GENERATION (4G) ROAD PROGRAM

The Colombian government is currently undertaking a huge project to improve the highway system, under the name of "Fourth Generation Highways", with the intent of updating major roads to international safety and speed standards. This $23 Billion USD program aims to expand the country's road network with 45 new highways, adding 5800 km of newly paved roads.

So, while it seems that bringing the 21st-century into Colombia could be impossible – it really isn't. Eventually, even this insanely rugged wilderness will be tamed by humans and the essence of the country will be forever changed.

↑ Father & son on rentals, said "This is the best ADV riding I've ever done"

↑ Medellín is the perfect place to start a motorcycle trip

Renting

GOOD FOR SHORT TERM TRAVEL

If you're planning on riding for a short period of time (from a few weeks to a few months) then renting may be the best option even if it may be a tad more expensive than shipping and/or buying. Why? Because shipping is time-consuming (both to and from) and puts your beloved bike at some risk. Your bike will also have to leave long before you do (to give it time to arrive) and you will also need to spend time clearing customs. Buying is likewise time-consuming: just imagine the days spent picking out a bike, doing all the paperwork, getting SOAT insurance etc. What's more, you will also have the responsibility of selling the bike before you leave the following month. You'll be spending half your vacation buying and selling!

LOW COST

If you're traveling for a short time, you may pay more per day for a rental but you're not dealing with any of the responsibilities of ownership such as purchasing a bike, repairs, and selling. Renting is probably the best option for short term travel although be sure to read the fine print. Renting can get expensive if you're traveling for a longer period of time and is sometimes limited in distance and mileage.

LESS HASSLE

Some riders mistakenly believe that money and time are the main determining factor but, when it comes to adventure riding, that actually doesn't rate as highly as it may seem and you may want to consider the inconvenience of purchasing or shipping a motorcycle. Is it worth it? Well, you decide: an 8-week trip can easily become a 4-week trip after losing a few weeks due to the logistics of purchasing a motorcycle in a foreign country. We'd say anyone planning a 3+ month trip ought to buy one locally – other than that, it's just better to rent.

It's also good to take into account the fact that by renting you get the help of the rental company owner who can give you helpful tips, help you out in choosing routes, help with hotel arrangements and help you out if you have a problem on the road. If you're not renting then you're on your own and you don't have any contact in the country to help you with all that.

Motorcycle Tours

INDEPENDENT VS. GUIDED

One of the most important choices you'll have to make when planning a motorcycle tour in Colombia is whether to take an independent (self-guided) tour or take a local and experienced guide along for the ride. There are pros and cons to both types of tours, of course, and although some may be obvious, others may elude you – this is especially true if you've never taken a motorcycle tour of any kind in a foreign country before. Here's a quick overview of what each option entails:

INDEPENDENT

Self-guided tours are an excellent choice for those with riding confidence and a little mechanical know-how.

When you explore a nation renowned for friendly locals, great riding conditions, and nearly-endless route options, touring is simply enjoyable – you're bound to have some off days, of course, and a flat tire will never make anyone's day – but this is very much a country that packs an awesome punch and offers huge rewards for all the effort.

Plus, you're not really doing it alone when you rent a motorcycle. Just because you're riding alone, it doesn't mean you'll be left to your own devices completely. It's not like we're going to hand you the keys, take your money, and shove you out the door! We're always happy to talk about routes, options, highlights, riding times, and everything else you'd like to know before you take off.

And, once you're out there, know that we are only a phone call away. Anything you need? We're (virtually) there! This is the kind of priceless help that makes renting a great option for short-term and first-time visitors.

THE PROS OF SELF-GUIDED TOURS:

Independence
Do what you want, when you want, and how you want to do it. This is probably the best reason to go off on your own. Come and go as you wish – get up late, or super early, change directions,

↑ A group getting ready to head out from Guatapé

A group riding near Sonson, Antioquia.

> A bike that's lightweight isn't just easier to handle whilst riding but also at slow speed (the trickier part) and when backing up into tight parking lots.

stop where you like, when you like, and for however long you like.

As guided as you'd like
Tour companies can recommend hotels to stay, restaurants to feast in, wonderful places to see, and activities to do along the way, offering a great compromise. This is, after all, our neck of the woods so it's only fair we share all our knowledge with you to ensure you have an unforgettable time. We can help as much or as little as you like – that kind of freedom can be priceless for the independent rider.

You choose your riding companions
We may well be great company (really, we are!) but you may also want the freedom to ride with those you know and love – friends or family, or even on your own. Lone rider?! We hear you!

THE CONS:

You need to be self-sufficient
We may be just a phone call away but that doesn't mean we can solve all your problems, as you face them. You should know the basics of motorcycle maintenance (because that flat tire won't change itself, unfortunately) and you do need to have the confidence to make last-minute changes, deal with road closures, etc.

You can't panic or stress easily
If you know that a small inconvenience can send you into a flurry of anxiety then a self-guided tour may not be the best option for you. Out there, you'll only have yourself for backup if anything happens, so you need to be level-headed and not prone to panic.

Some Spanish knowledge is good
Yes, we've had plenty of riders who've enjoyed independent touring without knowing a smidgen of Spanish but they are also the same ones who didn't encounter any problems or emergencies on tour.

GUIDED TOURS

The simpler, most convenient, and in

JEFF & ALAN'S GUIDE TO MOTORCYCLE TRAVEL IN COLOMBIA

↑ Paul and Chuck exploring the mountains outside of Medellín.

many ways more enjoyable option, the guided motorcycle tour can be the most genius combination of all: you get to experience a wicked motorcycle trip in this phenomenal country BUT you don't have to deal with ANY of the logistics.

If you're short on time but BIG on dreams then this option is perfect.

Guided tours allow you to truly enjoy Colombia in style, safety, and stress-free comfort. There's nothing wrong with finding fun trails on your own if you have the time and resources but riding with a guide means you'll enjoy the best trails, hand-picked to suit your riding ability, maximizing your time in the saddle.

Because every single time someone gushes about an amazing off-road trail, they fail to mention the 24 dead-ends that simply wasted their time.

THE PROS OF GUIDED TOURS:

You'll see and do more
There's no wasting of precious holiday

time when you're on a guided trip. All you really need to do is saddle up and enjoy, we take care of all the rest. If you only have a short vacation time and want to squeeze as much adventure as possible into your journey, a guided tour can be a real life-(and trip)-saver.

You don't need to be a motorcycle mechanic
Not confident that you can handle the bike's maintenance or any potential problems on your own? A guided tour means there is always someone to help you out if you get stuck or broken down.

It's OK if you don't speak Spanish Your motorcycle tour guide is your translator on the road and you'll no doubt learn more Spanish this way.

Best Food and Hotels
You'll eat at local's favorite places and stay in the best hotels that also offer fantastic value for money – guides know the places they visit, eat, and overnight in so you'll get better and more personalized service too.

Lighter and Safer
Carry less, enjoy more, and be even safer when you take a guide along for the ride. Enjoy that priceless confidence that comes from knowing someone else is taking care of all the logistics.

Interesting routes
We prefer to put you on smaller and more interesting local roads (with lots of twists and turns) but are always happy to create a personalized route for adventurous riders.

Comforting company
Sometimes, you just can't find anyone to go with you and that's a bummer. Never mind, though, because having a guide means you can have companionship, and aloneness, whenever you like. A guide isn't just a great source of comfort in times of need but they're also there for companionship if you're traveling alone. Ride out of Medellín with a guide and you'll have an instant 'local' friend that speaks your lingo and is there to make your experience even more rewarding.

THE TRADE-OFFS:

You'll spend more
Personalised and guided service will cost you more than if you were to go on a self-guided tour, which is to be expected since you have to pay for the guide as well as their motorcycle, gas, food, and lodging.

You may communicate less with locals
If your Spanish isn't up to scratch, you're likely to fall back on your guide which may also hinder your contact with locals. Although if you have a good guide you may have more contact with locals because they will engage them much more.

You may find it hard to let go of all the controls
You may find that some guided tours are too structured for your liking.

↑ The "Switzerland of Colombia" is only an hour outside of Medellín

What's the best type of motorcycle to ride in Colombia?

SMALL, LIGHT AND NIMBLE

Small, light, and nimble is the way to go and this country seems like it was absolutely tailor-made for small adventure motorcycles.

Aside from being affordable to buy, rent, and repair, small bikes are easier off-road, can be easily picked up by just about anyone, and are comfortable (and powerful enough) for long, multi-day tours. All of this makes the kind of motorcycles we offer (high-quality, lightweight, dual-sport/ADV) an absolute blast to ride.

Motorcycle touring should be FUN, first and foremost. We strongly believe that small, light, and nimble motos are better almost anywhere in the world and especially when riding through the mountains of Colombia.

Here are some other cool pros of riding smaller, dual-sport wheels:

Slow Speeds

Colombia is a land of twists and turns and, even if you had the most powerful adventure bike, the chances you'd ever take it past 100kph are minimal. This is especially true if you wish to ride up the Andes or get off the main drag at any time. Riding a BMW 1200GS in Colombia is like taking a Ferrari for a mad spin around a twisty go-kart track – given you'll barely break 30km/

JEFF & ALAN'S GUIDE TO MOTORCYCLE TRAVEL IN COLOMBIA

↑ My friend Alan riding his DR650 just south of Medellín

hr…what's the point? Just an expensive overkill, in our humble opinion, and not a fun one at that.

Zippy & nimble
Lane-splitting is legal in a lot of places in Colombia and given that most lane-splitting happens with heavy traffic, it makes sense that a smaller bike would be ideal. Weaving, turning, and overtaking is a breeze on smaller bikes and they are particularly nimble where you need it the most, in heavily congested cities. A bike that's lightweight isn't just easier to handle riding but also at slow speed (the trickier part) and when backing up into tight parking lots. Doing that on a heavy bike can be near impossible.

2-Up
Riding with a passenger is no problem for these bikes. The 300cc motors have more than enough power to get you and your passenger where you want to go.

Flat Feet
Smaller motorcycles allow you to comfortably and safely put both feet

> We strongly believe that small, light, and nimble motorcycles are better to ride almost anywhere in the world and especially when riding through the mountains of Colombia.

flat on the ground when coming to a stop – an absolute must if you're not all that confident on two wheels and, to be honest, excellent to have at any time you take a bike off-road.

Perfect for group tours
These bikes are also great for group tours if you have riders with varying levels of skill. Always remember that, when riding as a group, you're only as fast as your slowest rider.

Fuel-Efficient
Smaller motorcycles are extremely fuel-efficient and get around 60mpg / 25km/lt, which helps you save money during the trip. Some of our day trips take us into the backcountry of Colombia and, oftentimes, the fuel cost for the entire day is only $3USD!

Easy to pick up
Ever tried to pick up a 1200GS after you accidentally dropped it? You're probably still trying. Small adventure bikes are easy to pick up if you accidentally drop them. No rider should ever be on a motorcycle they can't pick up on their own.

Low-Cost Repairs
Maintenance and repairs for small adventure motorcycles are very economical and can save you a small bundle on the road if you're going at it alone. For many adventure riders heading our way,

↑ A DR650 in the páramo with a view of Nevado del Ruiz volcano.

> The Suzuki DR650 is simple, durable, reliable, and basically invincible. The DR's simple reliability is legendary. Keep it maintained and it will run for a LONG time without issues.

↑ The Colombian Police use the Suzuki DR650

saving money is one of the biggest priorities.

Low-Cost Insurance
Insurance for these motorcycles is way less than the larger ADV bikes. For Colombia, we highly recommend:

SUZUKI DR650

This single-cylinder, dual-sport Suzuki classic is a fantastic overlanding bike. Call it a bush pig, tractor, a tank, or whatever other names you can think of, there's no denying this is a solid choice for motorcycle touring, especially in Colombia, where they're used by the police - so finding spares and decent mechanics is easy enough.

Good fuel economy, a super comfy seating position, and excellent resale value (should you buy one here and wish to resell it before going home) make this the best choice of 'big' bike with which to explore Colombia. Although the bike has a high seat, origi-

↑ The DR650 is simple, durable, reliable, and basically invincible

nally, it can be greatly lowered and so is favored by anyone with shorter legs

Simple, durable, reliable, and basically invincible, even the most hardened adventurers get a misty glow in their eyes as they start talking about their next great overland journey, straddling their trusty DR650. Although it doesn't have the prestige of the popular European brand that begins with a B and ends with a W, it's definitely one of the most awesome bikes out there. The only thing missing is a gas gauge but that's true of many adventure bikes.

HERE IS WHY THE DR650 IS SO AWESOME:

Extreme Durability and Reliability
The DR's simple reliability is legendary. Keep it maintained and it will run for a LONG time without issues. In fact, there are numerous reports of DRs with over 100,000 miles on them. Simple air cooling is used, with an external oil cooler on the right side to take away engine heat. This reduces weight and eliminates the need for a water pump, thermostat, plumbing, a radiator, and fan (all of which are subject to damage and failure) and is what makes this motorcycle reliable almost to a fault. No fuel injection, no fancy techy stuff: just a fantastic old-school bike that's reliable and easy to fix.

Neck Snapping Torque
You're going to be surprised at how much power the single-cylinder produces. The torquey engine has 39.8 lb-ft of torque and is rated at 43 horsepower and has plenty of oomph for accelerating and climbing grades. It does surprisingly well at highway speeds: 80 mph (please don't drive that fast) is comfortable, and top speed is north of 100 mph (please don't ride this fast either). That being said, the torque isn't so much for the bike to get away from you if you accidentally drop the clutch or pin the throttle but it's definitely enough for a fun ride.

Long Distance Touring
In everyday riding, with a combination of freeway and local roads, mileage is around 50.5 mpg, which gives you a range to empty of around 150 miles using a stock fuel tank. On the open dirt roads, the DR650 is great on fuel, even if you are a little throttle-happy. This is not a racing bike, but I can tell you that I have NO trouble getting onto the freeway and it will cruise at 80-85 m/h all day long with no complaints.

Aftermarket Parts and Support
The current version of the DR650 was released in '96 and has gone largely unchanged since then. So, there is a huge selection of replacement parts as well as a plethora of aftermarket parts.

Larger gas tanks, custom seats, engine armor, luggage racks. Just about anything can be found to be added to make it exactly the way you want it.

Simple and Easy to Fix

Besides being a great "first-time adventure travel" bike, the DR is also a great "first-time mechanic" bike. If your DR is like most others, there really isn't a ton of maintenance beyond regular oil changes, occasional new spark plugs, etc. They are incredibly easy to work on when compared to any other motorcycle. The bike has very few parts and fewer parts mean fewer things to wear out, fewer parts to break and fewer parts to replace. Even better is that all of the parts are right there out in the open so if you actually happen to break something the whole bike can be stripped down to the frame very quickly. Also, no proprietary screws needing special tools to remove and no special factory only parts assemblies like on a BMW adventure bike. This is what makes the DR worry-free and easy on the wallet during a long trip through South America.

Resale Value

You probably aren't ever going to want to sell this bike but when you finally decide to go back home, whether that's in a few months, or a few years, the DR will have a high resale value and you'll probably be able to sell it for what you paid. Some people advise against customizing the bike to your liking and say that it decreases the resale value. This couldn't be further from the truth and half the fun of owning a motorcycle is getting to pick out the farkles (aftermarket accessories) and customizing it the way you want. Honestly, if you really want to have a good resale value, we recommend staying up to date with your periodic maintenance and keeping an accurate maintenance log with receipts.

RECOMMENDED MODIFICATIONS AND FIXES:

Auxiliary Lights

The front headlight on the DR650 isn't really that bright. You may want to replace the headlight bulb and/or add some low-cost auxiliary driving lights. It's worth taking a look at the 10,000 lumen Cyclops 10.0 H4 LED bulb. If you're interested in high quality, high power auxiliary lights we recommend checking out Ridgid, Baja Designs, or Black Oak LED light pods.

Neutral sending unit (NSU)

This is a sensor within the engine that lights the "neutral" indicator on the dash and is held in place by two screws. There are very rare instances where these screws have backed out and fallen into the engine. The root cause of this is that the screws are tightened against the plastic body of the switch. I'm sure everyone can imagine the carnage if one of those screws managed to bounce between a connecting rod and a crankshaft lobe at 5000rpm. A magnetic oil drain bolt may go a long way to catching a stray screw before it has a chance to cause significant damage. It's also advisable to use safety wire and Loctite to secure the NSU bolts.

Double sealed wheel bearings

The stock wheel bearings are only sealed on one side. If you ride off-road, these bearings could prematurely fail on you and result in ruined hubs. The first time you change your tires, get proper double-sealed bearings

The factory screws of the Neutral Sending Unit (NSU) can loosen over time but its an easy fix with safety wire.

> The starter of the DR650 is known to make a "squark" or rooster call noise when started.

in these sizes. We recommend SKF Explorer RSH bearings.

Squarky starter motor

The starter of the DR650 is known to make a "squark" or rooster call noise when started. This is due to moisture displacing the lubricant and creating dry bushing in the outer end cap. To fix this, simply, take the end cap off the starter, grease the bushing, refit. Make sure that the starter O-rings are in good condition since old or broken O-rings can allow moisture to make its way inside. Another way to fix this

↑ This Honda 250 Tornado went from Medellín to Ecuador, Peru and Bolivia

issue is to purchase a Warp 9 starter end cap which uses a billet starter cover with a sealed ball bearing.

HONDA TORNADO 250

The best lightweight adventure bike out there. Some state that this 250 doesn't do 'anything perfectly' but, to us, they're ideal because they manage to do everything really well. When you're planning a motorcycle tour through such a diverse country of Colombia, a jack-of-all-trades-bike is precisely what you need.

The Tornado was manufactured in Brazil and that makes it a very popular (and easy) bike to buy, rent, repair, and resell in Colombia. At just 134kg (dry), this is an easy bike to pick up and ideal for beginners who don't want to overwhelm themselves with a hugely heavy (and hugely powerful) bike, intermediate riders who just want to ride a fun, user-friendly bike, and anyone on a tight budget.

There's no denying that finding the right adventure motorcycle is all about compromise and we think the Tornado is what happens when you make the right choice. Forget about having the 'best bike in the world' and concentrate more on having a ton of FUN out there, on a reliable, light, fast little Tornado.

HERE'S WHAT THE TORNADO 250 OFFERS:

User friendly and easy to ride
The lightness of the Tornado is one of the most enticing aspects and can't be stressed enough. The bike is very lightweight and easy to maneuver. In the event that you do drop the bike, it's easy to pick up and you won't be at risk of getting hurt while standing it back up. The Tornado's engine also sports a flat torque curve and lower horsepower than larger touring bikes. This makes it a lot easier to control in slippery conditions.

Easy to find and inexpensive

both bikes and spares – as mentioned above, the Tornado is insanely popular in South America and that can save you a lot of time, and money.

They're (almost) indestructible –
Of course, you can run your Tornado to the graveyard but, if you treat it with TLC, there's no reason it can't dish up over 150K km – and then some.

Large tank
With almost 12L of fuel in a tank, you can churn out hundreds of km (over 300) on Colombian roads before you need to fill up. If you think you'd like to only fill up every 500km or so, then strap a fuel can to the back and off you go.

No fuel injection!
Picked up some dirty fuel? You can pop out the carburetor, give it a good clean, and be on the road again in an hour.

Basically a dirt bike with a comfy travel-friendly frame
Honda tries to fool you with the good looks of the bike, but the frame's rear

JEFF & ALAN'S GUIDE TO MOTORCYCLE TRAVEL IN COLOMBIA

↑ The XRE300 is the replacement of the Honda 250 Tornado

handles make packing for a trip a breeze. Make no mistake: this is an adventure bike that's perfectly suited to long-distance touring.

Great resale value
While we can't guarantee you'll make a profit from buying a Tornado, riding it for months, and reselling it, many riders do just that. Everyone loves these bikes so finding sellers and buyers is never an issue in South America.

RECOMMENDED MODIFICATIONS AND FIXES:

Ungreased bearings
It's always a good idea to grease the bearings on any bike you plan to take to the road but even more important on a Tornado, as Honda seems to have skimped on this part. Grease your swing-arm, steering column, wheel, and rear shock bearings with water-resistant grease. Also, consider replacing the single-rubber wheel seal bearing with double-rubber ones.

Weak headlight
Easy fix: replace the 35 watt -stock bulb with a stronger bulb. It's worth taking a look at the 10,000 lumen Cyclops 10.0 H4 LED bulb.

Sluggish at high altitudes
The only time the Tornado feels more like a light draft through a half-open window rather than a hurricane is when you're above 2,500masl, two-up, and fully loaded. We have met people who have taken the tornado through trips around South America while being totally loaded down with gear. Everyone we have talked to said that they performed fine. If they did encounter an issue at high altitude they simply opened up the airbox to allow the engine to breathe better. It's as simple as that.

No motorcycle is perfect but when you consider the value for money, the fun ride, lightweight and easy fix... the Tornado is pretty hard to beat in Colombia.

SATELLITE GPS TRACKER

If you're afraid that someone may try to steal your motorcycle, consider investing in a motorcycle GPS tracking device. These tracking devices use cell phone signals to send the current position of your bike to your cell phone. The tracker will also inform you of the motorcycles speed, direction of travel, and if the bike is currently on or off. You can get alerts and push notifications if the bike is disturbed and some apps even connect to Google maps to give you a 360-degree street view of the motorcycles current location. In an emergency, you can remotely shut off the engine via the cellphone app.

Buying & Selling A Motorcycle In Colombia

The XRE300 and Tornado 250 are lightweight and indestructible

Some motorcyclists planning on touring the country for a few months consider buying a motorcycle, riding it around, and selling it on their departure. It makes perfect sense if you're planning on riding for at least 4 months or more but it's a lot of work. Although it may seem cheaper to buy and sell, once you find out all the factors involved in purchasing and selling a motorcycle it may make more sense to rent. Many companies offer discounts for monthly rentals so before you purchase a motorcycle you may want to explore this option. There are a few questions we're often asked and we'll tackle them first before moving on to buying (and selling) a motorcycle here.

CAN I IMPORT A MOTORCYCLE TO COLOMBIA THEN SELL IT?

No. By law, foreign-registered motorcycles cannot be sold in Colombia.

If you're visiting Colombia with your own foreign-registered motorcycle, you can get a 90-day temporary import permit for the bike. The motorcycle needs to be out of the country when the permit expires. Remember, temporary import permits are precisely that: permission to bring your bike into the country for a short time only, on the promise that you will also take it out again

CAN I BUY A MOTORCYCLE IN COLOMBIA THEN SELL IT IN ANOTHER COUNTRY?

Also no. You won't be able to buy a motorcycle in Colombia and then sell it in another country. You can not buy a bike in Colombia and, for example, sell it in Argentina or the United States at the end of your trip. If you buy a motorcycle in Colombia to travel through South America you must come back to Colombia to sell it.

WHY ARE VEHICLES SO EXPENSIVE IN COLOMBIA?

Colombia charges up to 35% import duties on vehicles brought in from abroad depending on the country of origin. This means that you'll find cars and motorcycles here to be very expensive in Colombia and certainly more expensive than in the United States.

JEFF & ALAN'S GUIDE TO MOTORCYCLE TRAVEL IN COLOMBIA

How To Buy A Motorcycle In Colombia

- Register with the RUNT
- Find a suitable motorcycle
- Have an independent mechanic give the bike a thorough inspection
- Check that all the documents are in order Registration (matrícula), Vehicle Inspection (Técnico Mecánica), insurance (SOAT), and Taxes (impuestos)
- Transfer ownership
- Pay
- Check all your paperwork is in order...and ride into the sunset

Sound easy? Well, it's not. Without assistance, it will take you at least a week.

REGISTERING WITH THE RUNT

Every vehicle in Colombia is registered with the Registro Único Nacional de Tránsito. Also known as RUNT, this is a national traffic database that keeps track of vehicle and vehicle owners, detailing traffic infringements, accidents, insurance status, etc. When you buy a bike here, you will obviously have to update the vehicle's details, stating you as the new owner. This quick but important step should be done before you even start looking for a motorcycle.

You can and should register with the RUNT as soon as you've decided you will buy a bike in Colombia and having this task completed beforehand will make the ownership transfer go much faster, once you have found your dream ride.

Registration costs less than $10USD and only requires you to hand over your passport to the department of motor vehicles (called tránsito) so consider this the easiest part of the whole process.

At the office, you will have your photo taken as well as fingerprints of both your index fingers taken. Unless the system is down, you'll be done in about 15 minutes. You will also need to have a Colombia address so make sure that you have one.

You won't actually receive any kind of certificate or acknowledgment of your registration on paper but you can go online and retrieve your details at any time using your passport number – usually, it takes about 2 days for the details to show up, that's why it's important to do it first.

 **FIND A MOTORCYCLE**

As of 2019, Colombia had more than 8.9 million registered motorcycles. If you're starting your trip here you won't need to worry about a shortage of motorcycle sellers. You will find that lots of motorcycles in Colombia are in awful condition and that sellers aren't in the business of negotiating on the price, even when you point out the obvious faults. Don't worry too much though: bikes are cheap to fix and, if you find a good mechanic, they'll be able to strip the bike down and get everything fixed for a fraction of what it would cost in North America or Europe.

The most popular websites to start your search online are:

- MercadoLibre - Basically the eBay of South America

- OLX - On-line-exchange, a large classified ads platform

- TuMoto.com.co / TuCarro.com.co - Online listings for cars and motorcycles.

When searching these sites they will ask you for your location (ubicación) by state (departamento). Medellín is located in the department of Antioquia, Bogotá is in Bogotá D.C. and Cali is in Valle Del Cauca.

 MECHANICAL INSPECTION

I recommend getting an independent mechanic to look at the motorcycle you're interested in buying and remember that, here in Colombia, even the mechanic may not know what they are doing. They may just say the bike is all good because that's how he/she would ride it.

This is when it helps to really know something about bikes.

 **CHECK ALL DOCUMENTS - THE MOST IMPORTANT PART!**

Make sure you review all the documents that the seller provides!

MATRICULA / REGISTRATION CARD- First up, you'll want to check the VIN numbers on the frame and registration and make sure that everything matches. You should also ensure that the details of the seller match the details on the bike's registration card. Sometimes (actually, lots of times) people will try to sell a motorcycle that isn't

JEFF & ALAN'S GUIDE TO MOTORCYCLE TRAVEL IN COLOMBIA

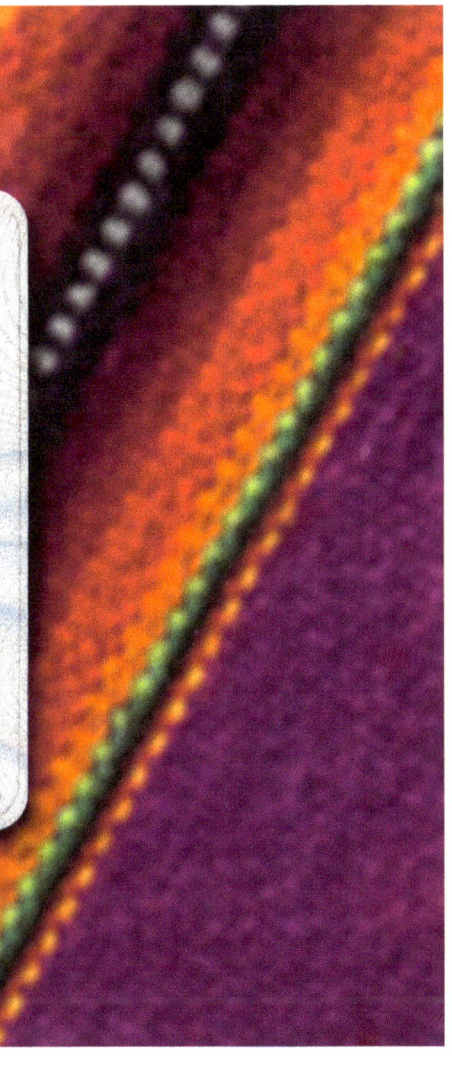

registered to them – it's not always sinister, mind you, most of the time it's because a guy is selling a family members bike or just helping out a friend. Don't hand over any cash until you've located the person whose name appears on the registration – make sure you meet the owner so you know it's a legit sale.

SOAT - Third-party liability vehicle insurance is mandatory in Colombia and is called the Seguro Obligatorio de Accidentes de Tránsito, or SOAT. This insurance is primarily intended for victims of traffic accidents - drivers, passengers, and/or pedestrians. SOAT will cover expenses such as emergency medical attention, hospitalization, surgeries, and rehabilitation.

All clinics and hospitals, regardless of whether they are public or private, are obliged to provide medical care through the SOAT.

SOAT is only valid in Colombia, and you are required to have this document on you at all times when riding.

This third-party liability vehicle insurance is mandatory. When buying a bike here, the most important thing to do is ensure the SOAT is valid. You can check it yourself, right here: https://www.runt.com.co/consultaCiudadana/#/consultaVehiculo

SOAT prices are fixed by the Colombian government. The prices are listed on the internet and are also displayed in offices that sell the SOAT policies.

CURRENT FEES – You can find the current prices for SOAT by entering the license plate of the motorcycle here: https://www.suraenlinea.com/v2/sura/soat/tarifas

SOAT insurance is transferred with the bike which means you can save yourself some expense if you happen to find a motorcycle with a lot of time left before it expires.

TAXES / IMPUESTOS - There are two main taxes that you need to check:

ANNUAL TAXES - All motor vehicles in Colombia are required to pay annual taxes with the tax rate varying depending on the state (departamento). The current tax rate for motorcycles in Medellín, located in the state of Antioquia, is 1.50% the value of the vehicle. Motorcycles below 125cc do not have to pay this tax.

TRAFFIC LIGHT TAX - Called "Semaforización", is a municipal tax that goes to fund well... traffic lights. This tax is used for the maintenance and programming of the traffic light system. In some cases, these resources are used to support and sustain the municipal transit secretariats. What does this mean for you? Just another tax that you need to make sure the seller has been

↑ Riding a motorcycle is the best way to experience a foreign country.

paid or else it's on you. Traffic light tax costs around $58,500 COP.

Make sure that all taxes have been paid. Some motorcycles haven't paid their taxes for years and if you don't make sure that the seller is up to date with the taxes, the registration of the bike will not be able to be transferred.

You can find out how much taxes are by following this link: https://vehiculosantioquia.com/impuestosWeb/

TECNOMECÁNICA

Técnico Mecánica or Mechanical Technical Review, is a mandatory procedure, which allows the authorities to know that the bike has been seen by a mechanic and is fully functioning to drive on the road. The SOAT and Tecnomecánica must both be valid at the time of purchase and at any time a bike is taken on the road.

On brand new motorcycles, the first Técnico Mecánica inspection needs to be done after two years and then it needs to be checked on an annual basis. Also, be aware that some red light and speeding cameras are also set up to see if your Técnico Mecánica inspection is up to date! If it's expired, you can count on getting a fine in the mail.

TecnoMecánica prices are fixed and are listed on the internet: http://www.ivesurcolombia.com/?page_id=396

> " Check on unpaid traffic fines before you buy your motorcycle or these fines will be transferred to you and it will be your responsibility to pay them.

TRAFFIC FINES

Just because you see all the documents are in order, it doesn't mean the bike is totally good to go. Unpaid traffic fines can really mess things up and lots of people have lots of unpaid traffic fines. If you don't check on this before you buy your motorcycle, these fines will be transferred to you and it will now be your responsibility to pay them. You can check for unpaid traffic fines and tickets here: https://consulta.simit.org.co/Simit/

IMPRONTAS - Rubbings or imprints of the bike's serial numbers, called "improntas", are needed for the transfer paperwork. Don't worry, this is easy to do.

You will need two things:

- Carbon paper, blue or black
- Transparent Scotch tape
- How to take imprints:
- Locate serial numbers located on the engine of the bike.

- Perform this operation with the bike off and with the engine cold to avoid burning yourself and melting the tape
- Use a degreaser to clean the area you need to imprint
- Place the carbon paper over the number and press down firmly so all the numbers are inked
- Take the tape and carefully place it on the number
- Rub the tape with your fingers while applying pressure to get the carbon to transfer to the tape
- Remove the tape, check that the number is completely traced and is legible

TRANSFERRING OWNERSHIP

The transfer process in major cities is quite straightforward and, as long as you take the seller along to make things speedier, it should only take you a day or two. If you are buying a motorcycle from a dealer, they'll typically take care of the paperwork although you will still need a RUNT registration which you will have hopefully already done, as suggested.

Here's how you transfer ownership of a motorcycle:

- Processing Request Form (Formulario de solicitud de trámite) - You will need to fill out a transfer form called "Formulario de solicitud de trámite", which costs just $5,000COP.
- Imprints (improntas) - You need to attach the imprints to the form
- Fingerprints (huellas) - How do you put fingerprints on the form? Use a "huellero" - a little ink pad, which you can buy for about COP 3,000. It's good to bring this when you go to sign the papers.
- Signatures (firmas) - Make sure the signatures of the buyer and seller match the way that they are the ID cards or passports.

This is when it helps to be really organized. At the transport office you will need to bring:

- Your passport
- An imprint of the chassis and engine numbers (details below)
- The bike's original registration papers (matrícula)
- The bike's third-party insurance certificate (SOAT)
- The bike's vehicle inspection certificate (tecnomecanica)
- Your address details (an AirBnB or hotel address will do)
- Details of the seller - It's a really good idea to take photocopies of the front and back of the ID card of the seller.

- Each municipality has its own transfer fees but they are generally in around $100,000 COP + 1% of vehicle value (if purchasing from a dealer, this cost will be included in the price – if buying privately, the cost is usually split between buyer and seller)

- Processing Request Form (Formulario de solicitud de trámite) - Complete with fingerprints, signatures, and imprints

- RUNT registration - This should already be registered in the transit authorities computer system.

If you have all your ducks in a row, it'll be a matter of walking into the office, filling out the transfer form, then handing in all your forms, paying, and, finally, collecting all your transferred papers. That being said, normally it takes a few days for all the paperwork to clear and actually get the bike in your name.

5 PAYING

Some sellers won't want you to drive away with the motorcycle until the paperwork is processed. This is because if you are driving the bike and get a speeding ticket or other traffic infraction, they are the ones who'll be stuck with the fine because the bike will still be in their name. Make it very clear to them that once you give them the money, you expect the paperwork to be done immediately. The last thing you want, on your end, is to leave a seller with your money AND the bike.

CASH

Most individual sellers will prefer to do the transaction in cash, although dealers will be ok with bank transfers. Cash still trumps transfers, at any given rate. Always deposit the money into the seller's bank account and get the payment receipt while at the bank itself. Do be careful when carrying around large wads of cash in Colombia. Make sure the bank and/or seller

> Once you give them the money, you will take the bike. The last thing you want, on your end, is to leave a seller with your money AND the bike.

gives you a receipt for your payment.

BANK TRANSFERS

Transferring money to a Colombian bank account as well as withdrawing large amounts of money from an ATM can also be troublesome because of daily withdrawal limits. We normally recommend using Western Union to transfer money from your home country and picking it up as cash in Colombia. Simply download the Western Union Mobile App and follow the prompts.

Make sure you have all the needed paperwork before riding away

Once the final payment has been made, make sure you have the Matricula, SOAT, tecnomecánica, and keys from the seller.

You're done!

← A "huellero" is a little ink pad used for adding fingerprints to documents

↑ Lightweight motorcycles can be easily transported with modified mototaxis.

Shipping A Motorcycle

Shipping a motorcycle from your home country to Colombia, or anywhere else for that matter, is pretty straightforward and you'll find an abundance of info on crating and shipping online. In this guide-book, however, I've decided to talk about a particular shipping challenge that is very Colombia-specific: shipping your bike from Panama to Colombia aka crossing the legendary Darien Gap.

THE DARIÉN GAP

The crossing of the Darién Gap is the single-biggest overlanding challenge in Latin America and the one hurdle everyone who's planning a Pan-American route from Alaska to Tierra del Fuego will have to tackle at some point.

> The crossing of the Darién Gap is the single-biggest overlanding challenge in Latin America.

To be honest, 'crossing' is a bit of a misnomer: 'by-passing' would be more appropriate terms to use.

WHAT IS THE DARIÉN GAP?

The Darién is a stretch of impenetrable jungle and swamp located on the border between Colombia and Panama. It's essentially the only gap along the 20,000-mile Panamerican highway that starts in Alaska and ends in Argentina. The gap measures just over 160 km (100 mi) long and about 50 km (30 mi) wide. Although the Darién's width varies along its length, the usual "gap" to which the name refers is between the town of Turbo in Colombia to Yaviza in Panama. When you plan a Darién Gap crossing, these are the A and B you'll essentially want to connect.

WHY IS IT DIFFICULT TO CROSS?

DANGEROUS - The Darién Gap isn't called the most dangerous place in the Western Hemisphere for nothing.

Since the Darién is the only stretch of land connecting the northern and southern American continents, it's used as a major drug-smuggling corridor and is controlled by armed guerrilla groups and narco-traffickers. Yet drug traffickers aren't the only ones crossing the gap. Illegal immigrants from all corners of the world including Iran, Sri Lanka, India, and parts of Africa, risk life and limb, oftentimes dying, while trying to cross the gap. Besides this, the Darién is almost totally uninhabited, so if you get lost or injured, you're on your own.

TREACHEROUS - Geographically, the Darién is a pretty rough place: impenetrable swamps, virtually impassable mountains, overgrown jungle, and unmarked trails are just a few of the highlights. Did we mention mosquitoes? Countless mosquitoes carrying diseases like malaria and dengue fever also inhabit the area. It's not surprising that the Darien doesn't really make the cover of many South American guidebooks.

WHY ISN'T THERE A ROAD?

The concept of connecting the Americas was first proposed in the early 1920s but due to the treacherous terrain talked about above it was written off as being almost impossible. Talks of road construction did stir up again in the 1970s, but the project never really took off – not only because of the obvious environmental impact on wildlife and native tribes but because it would be extremely expensive costing upwards of $300 million dollars.

Another contributing factor is that Panama is afraid that creating a road to Colombia will invite problems from Colombian organized criminals into its territory. Panama is one of the few countries in the world that doesn't have a military and Darién Gap acts as a natural buffer zone between them and Colombia, limiting violence to the jungle.

HAS ANYONE EVER BEEN ABLE TO CROSS THE DARIÉN?

The first vehicular crossing was achieved in 1960 by a Jeep and Land Rover expedition sponsored by the Pan-American Highway Congress and the National Geographic Society. The vehicles were able to successfully cross but averaged a speed of only 220 yards per hour over 136 consecutive days. Since then there have been around 10 expeditions that successfully made the crossing using 4WD vehicles and 2x2 motorcycles. More recently a group of military veterans crossed the gap on modified motorcycles.

JEFF & ALAN'S GUIDE TO MOTORCYCLE TRAVEL IN COLOMBIA

How to Ship Your Bike Across the Darién Gap

Unless you're Rambo you can always try your luck at dragging, swimming, and swearing your bike across the impenetrable jungle. If this option doesn't sound all that appealing, you're only left with three reasonable ways to get across the Darién:

- Fly your bike on a commercial plane (most expensive, efficient & painless option)
- Share a shipping container with other vehicles (least expensive but more time consuming)
- Sail across on a Roll-on, Roll-off (RORO) boat (slightly cheaper than flying and way more fun, but also more time-consuming)

 HOW TO FLY YOUR BIKE ACROSS THE DARIÉN GAP

This is by far the most enticing option IF you have some cash to spare, are short on time, or simply wish to get the whole ordeal over and done with, as painlessly as possible.

HOW – With this easy-rider option, you can hop on two separate planes to bridge the Darién Gap, between Bogotá and Panama City – services fly in both directions.

WHEN – It's always a good idea to contact cargo companies and get quotes two months before your intended crossing but, logistically, you'll want to set a date about 3 weeks ahead of time.

WHO – Air-cargo companies like Air-Cargo Pack and DHL can wrap-up your bike on a pallet and fly it over. Meanwhile, you'll need to hop on a commercial flight on the same route.

HOW MUCH – Expect your bike's sightseeing flight to cost around USD 1,000 whilst your own flight will cost somewhere around USD 200.

HASSLE FACTOR – Frequent flights, pretty seamless service, and efficient to the max: flying across the Darién is by far the most convenient option. You won't get to travel with your bike and that's always a little disconcerting but your separation-anxiety will be eased if you remove all valuables from the bike and take many photos before handing it over to the cargo company. This will help you solve any dispute should the bike be damaged in any way.

 HOW TO SHARE A SHIPPING CONTAINER WITH OTHER VEHICLES

Dedicated social media pages are awash with riders and drivers seeking like-minded overlanders with whom to share a container and an adventure all over the world. With this option, you hook up with other riders/drivers, decide on a company, set a date, and follow the carrier's instructions. Since this can easily be the cheapest way to mind-the-gap, it's also the most popular option. Perfectly suitable for the rider who doesn't fancy his or her bike getting drenched by seawater for days on end, the container shipment is undoubtedly the safest 'cheaper' option.

HOW – Container shipments trawl the waters between Cartagena and Panama City and although logistics companies have offices around both ports, you'll want to have sealed a deal long before you arrive. With this option, you'll first want to get quotes on both 20' and 40' containers and then start searching for container buddies. By the time you have a decent group organized, you'll know which container option is the most cost-effective for you. Usually, it's best to let one person deal with the company and the paperwork (pick an organized and level-headed team member) and, if that's not you, enjoy not having to do very much at all except send your leader

the required paperwork, pay your share and show up at the port on a set date. Sharing this process with others can be immensely comforting, most especially if you've never shipped your bike before. Both cargo companies and customs will treat you as 'one unit' so you'd better be sure everyone's paperwork is up to scratch and that no-ones carrying anything illegal.

WHEN – You'll want to start this whole process about 2-3 months before your intended departure.

WHO – Ever Logistics has a decent reputation and organize container shipments between Panama City and Cartagena, as does Enlace Caribe

HOW MUCH – Container ships charge around USD 2,000 for 40' of space in a sealed container and this option can be great value-for-money if you manage to find enough container-buddies and you can all agree on a date. Good luck with that! 20' containers are usually only marginally cheaper (certainly not half the price) so find more people with whom to share a 40'! Usually, groups will work out a payment-split based on space needed – i.e., a car/camper pays as much as two motorcycles, or thereabouts.

HASSLE FACTOR – This is really up to chance and depends highly on how many expectant riders/drivers are around, heading in your exact same direction, at around the same time.

3. HOW TO RORO YOUR BIKE ACROSS THE DARIÉN GAP

ROLL-ON, ROLL-OFF (RORO) – It ain't ever that easy to roll a bike on or off a boat! Having said that, you can squeeze in a multi-day island-hopping adventure for the same price as a short flight so, with ample time, this option becomes the all-around crowd-favorite.

HOW – Find a small boat willing to take you across for a nominal fee, a few hands willing to get your bike ON the boat, and then just hope you don't sink. Alternatively, you can save yourself a lot of time by simply following in the footsteps of many bikers who continually use the same handful of gorgeous sailing boats and catamarans.

WHEN – There's no reason to delay contacting a ship or catamaran if you're 100% convinced you want to cross the Darién. In high travel season, this is a very popular option so start sending your quote requests at least 2 months in advance.

WITH WHOM – Stahlratte, a centenarian schooner that's carved out a new life for itself as a motorcycle carrier, is one of the most popular options, alongside Wild Card Sailing, that offers a 5-day sailing experience which includes a meander around the San Blas Islands – hard to pass up!

HOW MUCH – You'll end up paying around $1,200USD for both you and your bike to sail across the Darién Gap.

HASSLE FACTOR – This one's just pure fun and can also be quite luxurious, depending on how much you're willing to spend. Oh, and unless you get awfully seasick or you're in some kind of a hurry. Still, you get a sailing trip AND manage to cross the Darién Gap in one delightful ride. Your bike won't appreciate the salt-water very much but give it a good wash on the other side and it'll be good as new.

Here's how you can also cross the Darién Gap:

 TOWN TO TOWN

The long way across...Turbo - Capurganá - Puerto Obaldia - Colón

If you have extra time you can hitch a ride from Turbo or Necoclí aboard a small cargo boat, bound for Capurganá. The crossing could take a whole day but you can also splurge on a speedboat ride that takes merely 2 hours. Spend a couple of days enjoying beautiful Capurganá before taking a one-hour longboat ride to Puerto Obaldia, Panamá.

Renowned as a budget traveler's Utopia (read: ramshackle village filled with crumbling homes and dodgy characters) Puerto Obaldia is a renowned drug-trafficking hot-spot, so as you may have guessed, it's filled with both scammers and heavy military presence.

The only real hurdle here is finding a boat to Panama via the San Blas Islands from Puerto Obaldia. Boats pass every 4-5 days so as long as time is on your side, it shouldn't be too stressful. The only issue people have is with Obaldia itself - it's not the prettiest town in the world (understatement of the century) and if you bore easily, this options isn't going to be for you

Once you do find a ride, you'll spend another few days aboard a boat, island-hopping the San Blas Islands with frequent stops ashore overnight and, before you know it, voila', you finally make landfall on the Panamanian mainland, usually in Cartí. But that's only if you're lucky. A popular scam leaves foreigners stranded on the San Blas, where you'll waste more time (and more money) trying to bridge the gap to Panamá City. Insist on paying at the end of your trip, not beforehand.

None of this is as easy as it sounds (and it probably doesn't sound easy anyhow) but hey, if you're after an adventure, this option will certainly deliver and should cost you no more than a few hundred bucks.

All up, it can take you up to two weeks to cross the Darién Gap this way, so consider this an adventure that is very much about the journey rather than the simple gap-bridging.

Sure, this may not be the fastest way to cross the Darién Gap but if you're looking for one of those 'stories to tell the grandkids', then nothing beats it!

MORE RESOURCES

Here are some social media groups and forums you'll want to join – here, you can search for updated info and fellow travelers with whom to share a container, as well as all sorts of other information about shipping a motorcycle

- PanAmerican Travelers Association on Facebook

- Horizons Unlimited – the world's #1 online travel biker's resource

Driving in Colombia

REQUIRED DOCUMENTS

If you want to ride a motorcycle in Colombia during your vacation, there are four main documents you'll need to have with you at all times:

- Your driver's license
- Registration papers
- Third-party insurance certificate
- Vehicle inspection certificate

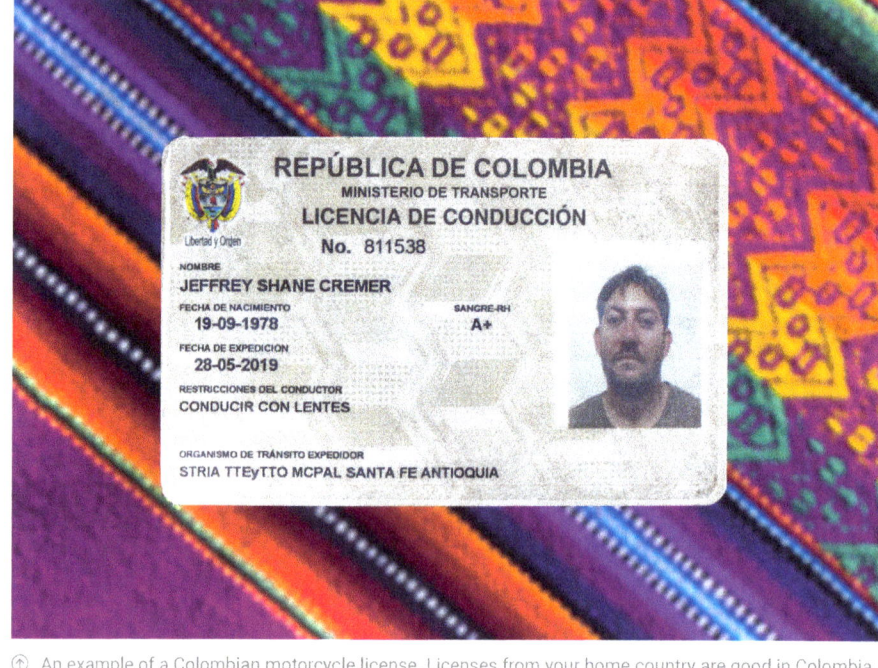

An example of a Colombian motorcycle license. Licenses from your home country are good in Colombia for up to 6 months.

Make sure you have all the necessary papers with you on every ride and don't be surprised if you get stopped for a check. It's not personal – cops just know that many riders in Colombia tour around without the necessary stuff (including license) so as well as being the law, it's kind of an easy revenue that's hard to pass up

LICENCIA - DRIVER'S LICENSE

According to the Ministry of Transport, foreign drivers are not required to have an international driving permit but it actually helps to have one. If staying in Colombia on a 90-day tourist visa (technically a tourist stamp), a valid foreign driver's license with a motorcycle endorsement is all that is needed. Always carry a copy of your passport and, if asked, show the page with your entry stamp. This will prove you're a tourist and, therefore, are not required to have a local driving license.

You need to have a Colombian residency to get a local driver's license. This is an arduous process and we're not even going to open up that can of worms here.

MATRÍCULA – REGISTRATION PAPERS

This will have details of the owner or seller, the vehicle number, engine, chassis, and model number. Whether you're buying, renting, or borrowing a bike in Colombia, always ensure that the bike's frame and engine number match exactly what is written on the matricula.

SOAT – THIRD PARTY INSURANCE

SOAT is mandatory 3rd party liability insurance and you must carry a copy of the active policy with you at all times.

Details of your SOAT – Make sure it's active and check the expiry date: https://www.grupor5.com/consultar-soat

TÉCNICO MECÁNICA

This is proof of road-worthiness. You should be well-acquainted with this by now – make sure your bike has been deemed roadworthy and has a valid Técnico Mecánica certificate.

REQUIRED GEAR

There are a few things you need to be able to ride legally in Colombia:

HELMETS – Want to get pulled over by the police in a millisecond? Ride without a helmet! Consider your brain an important body part? Ride with a helmet! All the time – no matter how short the ride. We always recommend a full-face helmet.

LICENSE PLATE NUMBER - Your license plate number must be displayed on the back of your helmet with reflective stickers. Most motorcycle shops in the country sell these stickers.

REFLECTIVE GEAR – Fluorescent vests are a must between 6 pm and 6 pm and they're generally a good thing to wear anyhow. If you're planning a lot of evening/night riding, then just wear reflective everything.

EMERGENCY TOOL KIT

Do you need an emergency tool kit? In one word: yep! If you're looking to do any type of off-road riding, we definitely recommend packing an emergency tool kit AND having the basic know-how to actually use it.

Luckily, we've put in endless miles while touring through the backcountry of Colombia and have learned a bunch of useful stuff along the way.

Here are our tips and product recommendations which we hope you'll find useful.

Everything should be small, lightweight, and inexpensive:

SMALL – Pack a huge tool kit that takes up half your backpack and, after day 4 of not using it, you may just leave it behind at the last guesthouse, accidentally-on-purpose. Make sure your kit packs small and fits comfortably in your bag.

LIGHTWEIGHT – Make sure your tools match the bike: everything should be lightweight and easy to handle. No point choosing to ride a lighter bike if you're gonna carry a 5kg spanner in your bag. Quick, simple, and lightweight is the way to go.

LOW COST - The cheaper, the better. An emergency kit should be just that: something you use sparingly in case of an emergency, not the kind of tools you need to swap the engine on your Triumph Rocket III. Leave the best quality, more expensive gear where it belongs (in your garage) and take their lower-maintenance cousins out for the ride instead.

We recommend assembling your own kit by checking out what sizes of fasteners (bolt and Allen heads, cross-head screws etc) your bike has and buying tools to fit. That being said here is a list of some items you might want to consider including in your kit:

WRENCH SET – Need to change a motorcycle tire or get some bolts off? We recommend a wrench set that's cheap, good quality, and small enough to put in your tool roll. If you're looking for a small socket wrench set you might want to check out the Cruz ToolsOM14 Outback'r Metric Multi-Tool

ADJUSTABLE WRENCH SET – To pick up where the metric leaves off.

MOTORCYCLE TIRE INFLATOR – Lightweight inflators can be extremely useful - the kind of ingenious tiny magical invention that can save you a ton of time whilst taking up no room at all.

TOOL ROLL - Make sure your tool roll fits all your gear yet packs small.

RECOMMENDED GEAR

RAIN GEAR & THERMALS – Wet weather and/or thermal gear may be lovely 'extras' to have on motorcycle tours in low-lying countries but, if you're planning to explore high-altitude roads in the Colombian Andes, they are absolutely essential for your survival. Hypothermia can be deadly. It doesn't even need to be that cold for it to be a safety issue. In fact, if you get wet and cannot dry at 50F (10C) you will not survive very long. If you don't remember anything else in this book, remember that fact. Your life could depend on it. Always carry rain gear.

KNEEPADS - Safeguard your knee-caps by buying a pair for $15USD when you arrive or buying riding pants with knee-pads sewn in. It's a small detail but even if you drop your bike at a low speed, if you hit your knee, your trip may be over.

GPS TRACKING DEVICE - GPS Tracking devices use satellite networks to transmit your location data to your friends and family to let them know that you are ok. In the event of an emergency, you can push a button and your location will be sent to emergency responders. Some GPS trackers can be used to send and receive short messages. We recommend taking a look at the Garmin inReach Mini, SPOT X, and SPOT Gen 4.

TIRE SPOONS – There are lots of different types of tire spoons out there but look for ones with good leverage so you can easily pop off the tire from the rim and smooth round edges so you won't puncture your tube when putting the tire back on.

ALLEN WRENCH SET - For portability, a folding set of hex wrenches is nice to have.

SCREWDRIVER SET – Small, simple, compact, and lightweight it's best to grab a simple reversible screwdriver with Phillips and flat blade options.

PARACORD - Paracord is lightweight, strong, and cheap and if it's good enough for military use, it's good

Garmin inReach Mini GPS Satellite Communicator - Enables two way text messaging using the 100 percentage coverage global Iridium network.

enough for us. Need to tow your bike? Do you need to tie down the lid of your top-box for whatever reason? This is the way to go. Keep 50' feet of it in a zip lock bag and you won't be sorry.

50L WATERPROOF DRY BAG - 30L is too small, 65L is too big – a 50-liter bag is pretty much the right size for a 1-2 week-long motorcycle trip in Colombia. Tie it down to the passenger seat with some Rok Straps and you're ready to go! You can grab an inexpensive duffle-bag from Walmart or splurge a little on a Touratech bag that'll last a million years.

ROK STRAPS – Another super useful item if you normally use bungees and ratchet straps to keep your bags in place. These are basically quick-release bungee straps. I only need to use two of them to strap my dry bag down and they're easy to take on and off the bike although they keep firmly in place whilst riding. Makes packing up a 10-second process.

Rok Straps

GORILLA DUCT TAPE - Duct Tape fixes everything. Recommended to have in your kit.

ZIP TIES - Can't have too many.

Pliers - You need these to remove the cotter pin from the axle nut. We recommend these more than needle-nose pliers because they have better grip strength and will do most of what needle-nose will do. Needle-nose pliers are nice for getting into super tight places, but that's not always going to be an issue on the road.

FLASHLIGHT - Don't rely on your phone for the flashlight, get a real flashlight or headlamp instead. We recommend flashlights with twist switches rather than push-button/click switches since twist switches are less likely to turn on in your pocket and be dead when you need it. Also, a push-button switch is more likely to wear out and fail over time than a twist switch. Stick with twist switches.

MULTITOOL - A multitool is basically a knife and emergency tools all rolled up into one. It's basically an emergency tool for emergency tools. Brands like Leatherman, Gerber, and SOG are popular among riders. We recommend checking out the Leatherman Surge, Skeletool and Sidekick are popular models.

High quality tire spoons are a must for any adventure traveler

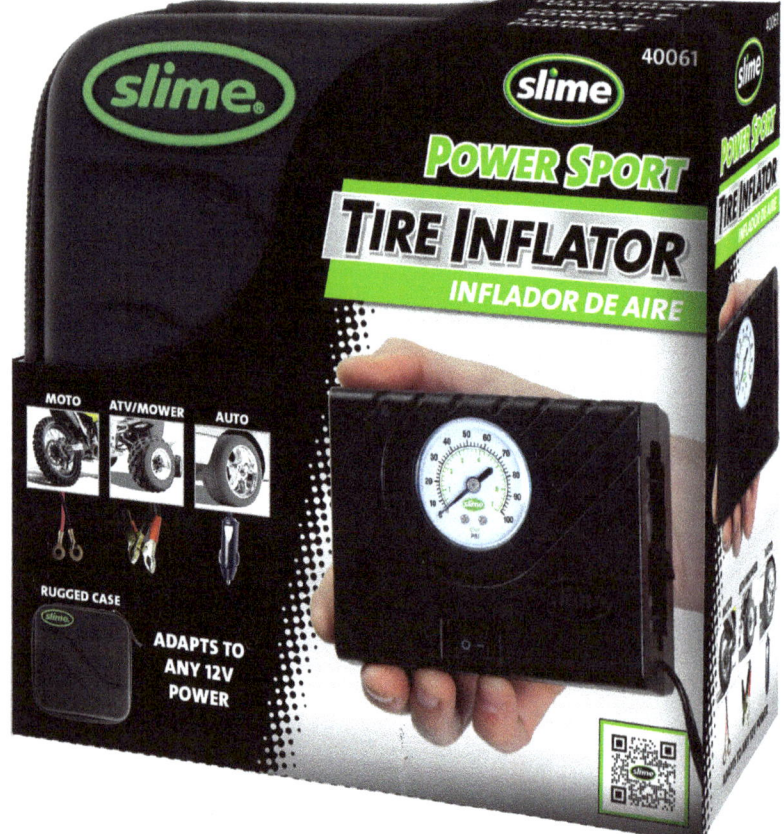

Small 12 volt air pumps make changing tires quick and easy.

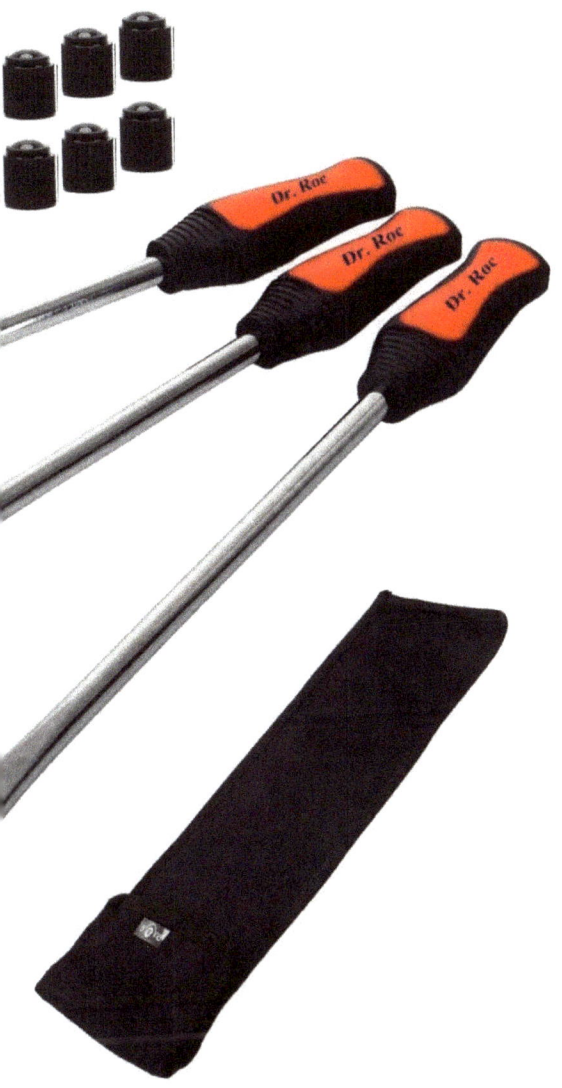

↑ Make sure to buy your SIM cards at the main branch of mobile operators

BUYING A SIM CARD

The most useful and versatile tool you can carry on your motorcycle is your phone. A runner up would be cash. The combination of those two can solve any problem. Convenient and inexpensive, prepaid SIM cards, like the one offered by Claro, can cost merely $10USD for one month's service and 2.5GB of internet access. The three main telco operators are Claro (market leader, the best in rural areas and the one we'd recommend), Movistar and Tigo.

SIM TIPS:

1. Buy your SIM in the main branches of each mobile operator, in authorized sites, or with insured retail providers - sometimes, dodgy shops will sell you a number already in use. Yes, eye-roll.

2. Make sure your phone does NOT have a SIM lock. Don't have an unlocked phone? You can buy a cheap one locally for $50-$80USD

3. Ask the shopkeeper to register the SIM card and configure it for you. Make sure it works before you leave the shop

4. You'll find cell phone retailers in every major mall in Colombia - do make sure you visit the official stores, rather than resellers, as you'll also get better service.

5. Topping-up your balance, called "recarga" (recharge), can be done anywhere that displays the logo of your service operator. Steer clear of street-side sellers if you can.

6. You usually don't need your passport to register the SIM card, but because it's Colombia, we suggest bringing a copy of your passport or your driver's license with you just in case they ask.

7. Make sure you ask for a prepaid card - only residents can get a post-paid.

8. Mobile phone shop locator for Claro: http://www.claro.com.co/personas/soporte/tiendas/

RAIN GEAR - Whether you love a full suit or prefer separate pants and jackets, it matters very little. Make sure your rain gear is comfortable and, most importantly, does the job. Don't forget waterproof gloves and make sure you have enough coverage on your neck, wrists, and ankles.

PLASTIC HOSE – Need to siphon gasoline? You'll need about 5 feet of 1/8" plastic hose for that delightful job. It's always good to get a clear tube to keep you from getting gasoline in your mouth.

TIRE TUBES / TIRE PLUGS - Among the most important spare parts you'll want to have. In an emergency, you can use a larger size front tire tube in the smaller rear tire. Also, don't worry about buying the bulky, expensive, heavy-duty tubes. The regular ones work just as well.

Driving Conditions in Colombia

Spend a day riding a motorcycle in Colombia and you'll realize that Colombian drivers do not try to avoid potential risks the way you might. Don't be surprised if a small motorcycle, traveling at a high rate of speed decides to pass you with just millimeters to spare – giving you no warning whatsoever and scaring you in the process. There's no denying that motorcycle riding in Colombia (especially in cities) can be challenging for the unaccustomed rider.

⊕ Imagine coming around a curve to this common sight in Colombia

Kids love to hang off the back of tractor trailers in Colombia

GENERAL CHAOS & MAYHEM

The second law of physics states that "No two objects can occupy the same space at the same time." This law barely holds true in Colombia – a country whose road use defies every law known to man. Imagine a road littered with cars and buses. In-between the cars there are motorcycles and, between those, are sellers pushing carts, serving up freshly squeezed orange juice. I even once saw a person standing in the middle of rush hour traffic selling plastic Roman gladiator masks.

The general chaos of many Colombian roads is an assault on the senses and this can be immensely distracting and overwhelming to the uninitiated. It can be very difficult to block out the fluff and concentrate on the riding but this is precisely what you must do to keep safe. Want to buy that gladiator mask? Pull over and park!

Here are just some of the biggest difficulties you're likely to face, in Colombia, as a foreign motorcycle rider:

LANE SPLITTING

Lane splitting is not legal in most of the United States because it's often a contributing factor in motorcycle accidents but, here in Colombia, lane splitting is legal in most areas and it's not uncommon to have three or four 125cc scooters flying between tractor-trailers at close to the speed of light. It takes a little getting used to and it's definitely something to be aware of.

HIDDEN COLOMBIAN SPEED BUMPS

Colombians call speed bumps "policias acostados" (laying down policemen) and you can expect to find them in excessive numbers all over the country – even where you'd least expect them, like in the middle of a blind corner (and we're not even kidding).

It may seem reasonable that towns along highways place speed bumps at their entrances and exits but wouldn't it be nice if they gave you the heads up?! They won't. If you're lucky, you'll pass a few communities who had enough funds to paint their speed humps yellow but, more often than not, they'll be nicely (and dangerously) camouflaged with the road. The shock you'll experience as you momentarily go airborne over a speed bump you didn't see is enough to give you a aheart attack so keep your eyes peeled.

ELUSIVE ROAD SIGNS

Road signs are used prolifically all over the country except where you'd really benefit from them – then they are nowhere to be found. Most of the time, you'll find road signage in Colombia to be self-explanatory but sometimes they can be a little confusing.

JEFF & ALAN'S GUIDE TO MOTORCYCLE TRAVEL IN COLOMBIA

HITCHHIKING CYCLISTS

Do you remember when you were a kid, riding a bicycle, and you'd tie a rope to the back of a truck to get a lift up a hill? In Colombia, there will be times when you'll see up to half a dozen bicycle riders literally hanging off the back of trucks. Remember to give this cycling-herd a wide berth and overtaking them swiftly and carefully: if one falls and ends up under your motorcycle tires, you may be in for some serious problems.

GRAVITY BIKES

Being towed by a truck uphill is apparently a lot of fun but not nearly as much fun as making a U-turn at the top and hurtling back down at breakneck speed. The moment you start tackling a steep uphill road, you'll need to keep your eyes open for maniacs on modified bicycles called gravity bikes. These kids can be seen dashing downhill and weaving through vehicles at speeds that sometimes exceed 100kph. Gravity riding claims a lot of local lives every year in Colombia and although the practice has been outlawed, it is still widely practiced. Once again: watch out for these guys because if you hit one, at your combined speeds, the consequences could be disastrous.

PAINTED LINES

For some reason, the Colombian government decided to use a kind of road paint that becomes super slippery when wet. Perhaps they were trying to deter the gravity bikes?! Pay special attention when changing lanes or generally riding in wet conditions.

LIVESTOCK

Expect to share the road in rural areas with cows, donkeys, horses, or dogs.

NO HEADLIGHTS

Some motorcycles, as well as busses, cars, and trucks, drive down the road with no lights on, even after dark. Others may be in front of you at night with only one signal light flashing, making them almost impossible to see.

WRONG-WAY

Not every driver in Colombia is drunk at the wheel even though it may seem like they are. Most of the time, they're just swerving to avoid potholes or choosing the best side of the road to drive on – yes, even if that means driving on the wrong side of the road. Time to ride defensively and pull out all the stops: use your high-beam and horn to get their attention (in case they're so busy watching out for potholes that they don't even see you coming), slow down, and pull over as safely as you can. We don't recommend you also swerve to the wrong side of the road to avoid them, however, as they are likely to correct their position at the very last minute – and then you'll be in the wrong.

> The Colombian government decided to use a kind of road paint that becomes super slippery when wet.

FAMILIES WALKING IN BLIND CURVES

Women with strollers/prams as well as entire families can be found walking on the road or even across the road at the most dangerous places of all: blind curves. We've developed the habit of actually expecting walkers close to curbs on blind corners and riding accordingly. Slow down, scan the roadside and take the corners a little wider, and both you and them will be fine.

SINKHOLES

Another interesting road hazard in Colombia is the sinkhole, which is basically a pothole on steroids. These humongous holes in the asphalt are oftentimes unmarked but, sometimes, they'll be marked with a tree branch or pile of bricks.

PARKING ANYWHERE

People routinely park on roundabouts and below overpasses. They also make sudden random stops in the middle of the road. Need to answer the phone? Just stop in the middle of the road. Need to get directions? Just slam on the brakes and stop. Be careful of random unattended vehicles as well as sudden stops.

↑ Washing machine rental is big business in Colombia. The washing machines are delivered to clients via motorcycle

ColombiaMotoAdventures.com

World-class adventure riding in Colombia

THE BIGGEST DANGER: YOU

The single biggest factor that'll determine your safety on the road in Colombia is the way you ride.

Colombian roads may sound like a complete nightmare but this is actually how 80% of the world actually works. Chickens, cows, and donkeys on the road, pushcart orange-juice-sellers, swerving motorists, and sinkholes half the size of Manhattan are the norm on most of the world's roads.

Take into account that the landscape is pretty flat in places like Texas and Florida and you may not be used to all the twists and turns that Colombia has. This is another reason why we recommend using smaller, easy to maneuver motorcycles for trips around the country.

All this being said, the real risk while driving in Colombia are the same risks that you face back home with most accidents being easily avoidable if you simply slow down and pay attention while riding.

Here are some common riding issues you'll want to avoid:

CARS MAKING LEFT-HAND TURNS - Motorcyclists are most in danger of an accident when a car is making a left-hand turn. About 42% of all traffic accidents involving a car and motorcycle involve a car turning left. Make sure to pay attention when coming to an intersection and try to predict the movement of other cars as best you can. Don't be afraid to use the horn as a precautionary measure when riding through an intersection, passing a car that might not see you, or going around a blind corner.

ALCOHOL USE - About half of all single motorcycle accidents are caused by alcohol or speeding so save the good times for when the day's drive is over.

EXCESSIVE SPEED - No reason to rush when there is such beautiful scenery. Want to avoid sliding out on gravel in a corner? Want to avoid getting freaked out by accidentally entering a corner too fast? Slow down and ride at a pace where your reaction time and ability to take action fit within your range of vision.

DISTRACTED DRIVING - With mobile phones, GPS, and other modern conveniences, distracted driving accidents are more common than ever before - 20% of all injury crashes involve some form of distracted driving. When you couple that alarming statistic with drivers who don't share the road with motorcyclists, it leads to dangerous – and sometimes deadly – results.

COUNTERSTEERING - We strongly recommend reading about countersteering. Countersteering is the technique you consciously or unconsciously use to turn the bike. In short, you push left on the handlebars to go right, and vice versa.

Local Knowledge

SPEED LIMITS & SPEED CAMERAS IN COLOMBIA

If you go by what local motorists do, you may be fooled into thinking that speed limits, in Colombia, are totally optional. They're not!

Here are the speed limits you should be aware of, as well as the distances you should keep from the vehicle in front of you. It's a good idea to memorize them given there may not be any road signs to alert you of changes:

- Schools/residential – 30 Km/h
- Urban – 60 Km/h
- Rural – 80 Km/h
- Motorways – 100 Km/h

SPEED CAMERAS

These are the reasons why knowing the speed limits in Colombia is really important. Whilst road signage can be a bit of a hit and miss, you can trust that speed cameras are not only abundant but also immaculately maintained. Fines can be hefty so unless you don't mind parting with $150USD for being just over the legal speed limit, keep your eye on your speed.

If speed cameras capture your image, expect to receive a bill for the offense by mail. It may take about a month for it to arrive, but trust that it will arrive. Nothing else arrives by post in Colombia but, miraculously, speed fines always do. Multiple statements may show up if you fail to notice the cameras on several occasions on the same stretch of road. I recommend using the Waze App to see

↑ Gas stations are full-service meaning that someone pumps your gas for you.

> Motorcycles don't need to pay tolls in Colombia. You'll see a dedicated motorcycle lane on the far right of the toll station that allows you to pass without paying.

where police checkpoints and speed cameras are located. The app will also advise you on the speed limit in the area.

HIGHWAY TOLLS

Motorcycles don't need to pay tolls in Colombia. You'll see a dedicated motorcycle lane on the far right of the toll station on highways, that allows you to pass without paying.

PICO Y PLACA

"Peak & Plate" is a traffic restriction system that Colombia introduced in the hopes of reducing congestion in larger cities. For the most part, alternating vehicles (by number plate - placa) during morning and evening peak (pico) times has worked in reducing emissions. The determining number is the first digit of your bike's plate and, if it matches with restrictions, it means you are not allowed to ride during allocated times.

The super-duper fun thing is that the numbers seem to change willy-nilly and are different depending on the city, so memorizing them is impossible. Restrictions can also change at the last minute so do yourself a favor: simply double-check with the relevant website before reaching your next big city.

Website: https://www.pyphoy.com

Twitter: https://twitter.com/Areametropol/status/1226243030971289600

MOTORCYCLE PARKING

Most malls and parking lots in Medellín provide separate parking for motorcycles and, while some charge, others are free. Each place will have a different procedure, but here are the basics:

TOLLBOOTH – Grab a parking ticket as you enter and present it, along with your payment, to a toll booth attendant at the exit gates.

PAY MACHINE – No toll booth at the exit gates? Feel free to waste half an hour locating a pay machine, insert your card, pay, grab a receipt and your parking card, ride to the exit gate, insert your parking card, and off you finally go.

FREE OF CHARGE – A few malls and parking lots do not charge motorcycles at all. However, you'll still have to grab an entry card, and, upon exiting, you'll have to give the card back AND show your motorcycle registration papers.

OVERNIGHT PARKING – If your hotel or guesthouse doesn't offer secure parking overnight, we always recommend you use a paid parking lot, instead of one that is either unmanned or free of charge. These parking lots, called "parqueaderos", are found everywhere and they are the safest option.

GETTING GAS

All gas stations are full-service meaning that someone pumps your gas for you. As is the case with most countries, you'll be asked to get off the bike to fill up the tank: this is to decrease the chance of people driving off with a full tank as well as for safety reasons, in case the bike catches on fire while it's being filled.

Here are the different fuel variants you'll find in Colombia:

- **CORRIENTE** – Regular low octane gas, usually around 87 Octane
- **EXTRA** – High octane gas, usually around 92 Octane
- **ACPM** (Aceite Combustible Para Motores) – Diesel
- **GNV** - (Gas Natural Vehicular) – Natural Gas

You can check the current price of gas, right here: https://www.globalpetrolprices.com/Colombia/gasoline_prices/

I normally ask them to fill it up with regular gas by saying "lleno de corriente".

Do you need to carry extra fuel on the bike?

Unless you're planning to spend a lot of time riding in extremely remote areas, this won't be necessary. There are gas stations all over the place and, where there isn't a gas station, you'll find hardware stores and random locals selling gasoline in plastic or glass bottles. Just ask!

WHAT TO DO IF YOU'RE STOPPED BY THE POLICE

During your travels in Colombia, you're sure to come across at least one police or military checkpoint. Most of the time, the police simply wave you down and ask to see your documents. They are checking to make sure you have a driver license, insurance, mechanical inspection (Técnico Mecánica) inspection, and registration. About 99.9% of the time, they'll just let you go on your way if everything is in order.

If they find due cause for a fine, you

Motorcycles don't pay tolls in Colombia and use a small lane located to the right of the toll booth to pass through

> Most of the time, the police simply wave you down and ask to see your documents. About 99.9% of the time, they'll just let you go on your way if everything is in order.

should be given a ticket and be told the nearest place to pay it. 'Some' members of the police force may ask you to pay an on-the-spot fine which, by the way, is not required. Now would be the time to use your good judgment: if it feels safe to refuse, do so.

Colombia is trying to stamp out corruption across all areas of government and is making progress in the police force but, every now and then, you will find a cop who needs a little extra money and causes a problem.

JEFF & ALAN'S GUIDE TO MOTORCYCLE TRAVEL IN COLOMBIA

EMERGENCY 123

Hopefully, you will never need to dial the emergency number in Colombia but if you do you can simply dial 123 on your phone to call an ambulance or the police anywhere in Colombia.

REPAIR SHOPS

There are almost 9 million motorcycles in Colombia. Cheap repair shops are everywhere so you're never too far from a mechanic or tire changing place. Unless you're in an extremely remote area you don't need to worry about being stuck without a mechanic.

Medellín has about 4 blocks of bike shops in an area of town called La Bayadera, right across from the Exposiciones metro station. Here, you'll find mechanics, motorcycle gear as well as spare parts and accessories (called lujos). You can also do Técnico Mecánica inspections, buy insurance, and take care of most motorcycle related paperwork in this area. They even have people on the street corners who can repaint your license plate and make it look new again.

Most motorcycles in Colombia are small, low-cost 125cc-300cc bikes so you may have parts available for these motorcycles even in smaller towns but, if you're riding a big BMW or KTM, you may only be able to find parts in large cities.

↑ Proper tools keep small problems from becoming big headaches.

ColombiaMotoAdventures.com

JEFF & ALAN'S GUIDE TO MOTORCYCLE TRAVEL IN COLOMBIA

Planning Your Own Route

WHEN IS THE BEST TIME TO VISIT COLOMBIA?

Colombia has two seasons: rainy and dry. We're not talking monsoons here. Rainy season just means predictable scattered afternoon thundershow-

ers. Still great for motorcycling, just bring rain gear. The rainiest months are April, May, September, October, and November. Around the Equator, temperature is regulated by altitude, and not by seasons. The lower the altitude, the warmer the weather. The higher the altitude, the colder it gets. When riding, it's good to consider the change in altitude when planning the ride since changes in temperature can be dramatic. You may start the day in a hot tropical climate but arrive in a cold mountain climate by lunchtime.

| Dry Season (Summer Season) | December - January, July - August |
| Rainy Season (Winter Season) | April - May, October, November |

TEMPERATURES BY ALTITUDE

Altitude	Temperature	City
Less than 1000m	More than 24°C (75F)	Cartagena, Santa Marta, Cali
Between 1000-2000m	Around 20°C (68F)	Medellín, Manizales
Between 2000-3000m	Around 14°C (57F)	Bogota, Pasto
More than 3000m	Less than 10°C (50F)	Nevado Ruiz

*thanks to Wikipedia

PLANNING YOUR OWN ROUTE
GOOGLE STREET VIEW

If you want to know the road conditions or current state of an unknown area on your route, Google Street View is one of the best route planning tools out there. Google Street View provides 360-degree interactive street-level panoramas from positions along streets and roads. If you want to zoom in from the map and see a 360 panorama photo of the area, Google Street View is the best way to do it. This is a great way to check to see if the roads are paved, gravel, mud, dirt, etc.

Zooming into Street View is easy. Simply, click and hold the yellow person icon in the bottom-right corner of the screen and drag it to the spot you want to view. As you move the cursor, called Pegman, over the map, the streets will highlight in blue or become blue dots. These are the areas where there is a panorama. Make sure that you place the icon onto one of those dots; otherwise, you won't be able to see the street view.

To navigate within the panorama, click and drag inside the photo to move the camera angle and look around. You can also tap a location down the street to move closer to it. It's kind of like virtually driving down the road.

iOVERLANDER

Described as an app built for Overlanders, by Overlanders, iOverlander is becoming a must-have app for adventure travelers. iOverlander compiles locations and reviews of places submitted by their community then displays the information on a map based on your GPS location. The app pretty much provides all the information for critical things when traveling in remote regions. Information about hotels, campsites, restaurants, mechanics, water, and many other categories are displayed. It even shows you where you can do your laundry. Details for each place are listed, including amenities, photos, date last visited, and GPS coordinates. iOverlander is especially helpful when looking at the areas of the map that don't have a lot of information listed in Google. There may not be a hotel or restaurant listed in Google, but chances are that at least one person has explored the area and posted it to the app.

MOTORCYCLE NAVIGATION IN COLOMBIA

Navigating around Colombia is pretty easy and we've made it even easier by equipping our bikes with cell phone holders and USB chargers. Just set up your route on Google Maps and off you go.

We realize there are multiple trip planning and navigation apps out there but, on the road, we mostly use Google Maps and Gaia, which we'll detail below. The most important aspect of any navigation app is that the maps are downloadable and readable offline – trust us when we say that the one time you will REALLY need help is the ONE time you have NO cell reception.

GOOGLE MAPS

Good ol' Google Maps: easy, intuitive, and very accurate. Saving locations in advance and downloading offline maps are very useful. I doubt any other app has more data and better functionality. It's also easy to switch between satellite and street map views. You can save an area from Google Maps to your phone or tablet and use it when you're offline. Google Maps was recently updated using a new "color-mapping algorithmic technique." This makes it easier to distinguish between natural features in the environment, whether they're mountainous ice caps, deserts, beaches, or dense forests which is a

huge help when navigating through a new country.

GAIA GPS

Gaia GPS is known as the "killer app for backcountry navigation" and basically turns your cellphone into a hand-held GPS unit. An important difference between Gaia and Google Maps is that Gaia is based on the OpenStreetMap data set. This is an important difference as the map data set does a better job of showing remote roads and trails that don't appear on Google maps. Besides the OpenStreetMaps data set, Gaia also supports a plethora of map overlays including topographical, street, outdoor, and aerial, which you can combine and adjust to make a personalized map. Another important feature is that Gaia, like Google Maps, supports the downloading of map sets so you can navigate without cell phone service.

PAPER MAPS

Let's not forget about paper maps. Paper maps can be a great alternative to GPS when your phone falls off your motorcycle and gets run over by the car behind you. Often, when we are navigating with GPS, the map is zoomed all the way in, and we forget to see the overview of where we are. Paper maps are also a great way to check out the country's general landscape and find new places to go. Paper maps are also cool. Try sitting around the fire with friends, looking over a bright GPS screen. It just ain't the same.

ACCOMMODATION

HOTELS

Colombia is undoubtedly one of the best-serviced countries in all of South America as far as accommodation is concerned – you'll find a huge array of lovely guesthouses and boutique hotels, even in remote locations. Check out Hostelworld for inexpensive hotels, all over the country. Airbnb has also picked up in popularity in recent years so, as long as you find suitable and safe parking for your bike, this is an excellent option when touring Colombia.

No matter where you decide to stay there are a couple of things that you should know about:

The Colombia Ministry of Tourism requires you to leave a copy of your passport at the hotel when checking in. Most hotels can make a copy when you arrive but you may want to email or WhatsApp them a copy or have copies already printed to save time when checking in.

Also, If you are a bonafide tourist, meaning non-resident, you are eligible for the exemption from the 19% VAT tax (IVA in Spanish) on the room rate.

HERE ARE A FEW OF OUR FAVORITES:

LOS PATIOS, MEDELLÍN – With guarded overnight parking, ideal location, rooftop bar, fully-equipped kitchen, high-speed WiFi, and coworking space, this choice is unbeatable.

61 PRADO GUESTHOUSE, MEDELLÍN – Inexpensive option with great amenities, a beautiful rooftop patio and views, a 24-hour restaurant, laundry service, and free parking. Perhaps not the best location but fantastic value-for-money. The owner is an architect and the hotel is beautifully designed on the inside.

DIEZ HOTEL, MEDELLÍN – A pricier Medellín choice with good parking, the Diez is in a central location near Parque Lleras and all the clubs in El Poblado. The sushi bar is fab!

THE CHARLEE, MEDELLÍN – Another centrally-located hotel with parking and unique interiors.

EL TESORO HOTEL, SONSÓN – Stepping into El Tesoro is like stepping back in time – a gorgeous 215-year-old hacienda converted into a hotel. One of the most unique hotels we've ever stayed in, the hotel is filled with an amazing collection of antiques.

TERMALES DEL RUIZ HOTEL, MANIZALES – We visit this place often on our tours and it's always a treat. This thermal bath complex is nestled amid spectacular high-altitude landscapes (3500masl – 11,500ft) and boasts an outdoor thermal pool is a luscious garden setting. Lots of hiking options and an ideal place to just kick back and relax.

HOTEL MONARCA, SALENTO– Stunning views of Salento and surrounding cloud forest valley. All-around and beautifully appointed rooms and an amazing deck for breakfast, dinner, or just hanging out. Hotel Monarca is perfect when visiting Salento.

MONTE TIERRA ECOHOTEL GLAMPING, FILANDIA – Monte Tierra offers sensational transparent dome glamping tents set in a jaw-dropping, nature-infused location, near Salento and the Cocora Valley.

CAMPING

Let's talk about camping. There are basically four reasons to camp:

YOU'RE IN AN EXPENSIVE COUNTRY - Everyone knows that traveling through Europe can be expensive. South American countries such as Chile, Argentina, and Uruguay are also expensive and you could save some decent money by camping.

YOU'RE IN A REMOTE AREA - Some places in South America are remote and hotels are few and far between. You have to have your camping gear in situations like that.

EMERGENCIES - Pitch a tent on top of a bed - bug net. An air mattress makes a bed on a deck, beach, ferry, and during long airport waits. A small sleeping bag is great if you're staying in a not so clean hotel room.

YOU LOVE CAMPING - This is the best reason to camp. If you really just like camping we say go for it!! After all, no hotel can compete with a great view from a tent in the mountains.

If you want to do a motorcycle adventure where lodging is cheap and plentiful then skip carrying all the gear etc, come to Colombia and get a room! We believe that camping isn't really necessary on a trip through Colombia:

IT JUST DOESN'T MAKE ECONOMIC SENSE - Rooms are cheap in Colombia. You can get a hotel for $20USD a night. If you're traveling with a buddy and you're sharing a room, the price is only $10USD per person per night. Do you really want to be camping out with the risk of getting rained on just to save $10USD per night? Meals are incredibly cheap too. How much money are you really saving by cooking on the campfire when for $5USD a restaurant cooks for you and does the dishes.

LOTS OF GEAR AND EXTRA WEIGHT - If you're in South America you pretty much have to commit to camping often enough to warrant carrying all the extra gear and weight.

RAIN - Even if you have a great tent, if it rains, things can be unpleasant. Think of packing up or setting up in the rain? Wouldn't you rather have a dry morning with a nice breakfast rather than starting the day cooking breakfast in unknown territory.

ONLY OCCASIONAL USE – After a long day´s ride, all that most people want is a good shower and a comfortable bed. Sometimes, occasional campers head our way and what they discover is that food and lodging are so cheap, they no longer need to go through the motions of setting up camp.

PRIVATE PROPERTY - Camping outside of designated areas and parks is not common, nor recommended. If you just plop your tent randomly on the side of a highway or rural area, then there's a good chance that you will be doing so on private property. As a good rule of thumb, we always ask permission to pitch a tent from the nearest farmhouse

Having said all that, there are plenty of gorgeous camping spots in national parks: spending a few blissful days soaking up the Colombian wilderness is undoubtedly the best (although some might say only) reason to pack a tent.

WHERE TO CAMP

There are just too many good camping spots to list. To help you search out good camping sites in Colombia, we recommend downloading the iOverlander app. iOverlander compiles locations and reviews of places submitted by a community then displays the information on a map based on your GPS location. The app gives more information than just camping sites, though, and includes information about hotels, restaurants, mechanics, water, propane filling, and many other categories. Details are also listed for each place, including amenities, photos, date last visited, and GPS coordinates.

The landsacape outside of Salamina

HOW MUCH DOES IT COST TO TRAVEL IN COLOMBIA?

BUENO, BONITO, BARATO

This question gets asked all the time. The prices in Colombia will vary like they do in any other place. We usually recommend a budget of around $55USD per day, excluding the cost of renting or buying a motorcycle. This budget will get you something that the Colombians refer to as BBB or Bueno, Bonito, y Barato, which means good, nice, and cheap. These are just regular accommodations and food that aren't too fancy but are safe, clean, centrally located, and have good reviews.

If you're interested in spending a little more for some more luxurious accommodations, you can check listings on Booking.com, and you may want to up the budget to maybe around $75-$100USD per day. After all, it's a vacation, and you can't put a price on happiness! We think that it's good to do a little bit of both: sometimes inexpensive hostels in some places while spending a little more every once in a while on unique hotels in beautiful places.

We can't give you the price for every hotel in Colombia or give you an exact budget for your trip. What we can do is give you some current prices for some regular expenses in Colombia.

> In rural areas you can expect the price of hotels to be one third the price of what you would find in the United States or Europe.

JEFF & ALAN'S GUIDE TO MOTORCYCLE TRAVEL IN COLOMBIA

 Local flavor takes on many forms.

FOOD

Restaurant prices are crazy cheap and the food is excellent. For example, going out to a good restaurant in Medellín that serves a great steak with wine will only run you around $30USD for two people. There are a lot of different kinds of food available as well. Italian, Mexican, Middle Eastern, everything that you find in cosmopolitan cities in the United States and Europe you will find here. A typical inexpensive lunch costs anywhere between $3 USD - $5 USD.

DRINKS

Colombian rum is cheap, especially if you are drinking Medellín 3 Años. A shot of rum will only cost you around $1 - $1.50 USD

Beer is also cheap and is only about $1 - $1.50 USD per bottle.

> Colombian rum is cheap, especially if you are drinking Medellín 3 Años. A shot of rum will only cost you around $1 – $1.50 USD

HOTELS

A good rule of thumb is that the prices of hotels in major cities in Colombia are about half the price of what you would find in the United States or Europe. In rural areas, you can expect prices to be around 1/3.

Cheap but good hostels, such as the ones found on HostelWorld.com, vary in price from around $25 - $35USD for a private room. Shared dorm rooms can be had for approximately $10USD per night. Boutique hotels in the coffee region can run from $50 - $75USD per night. The Movich Cartagena Hotel, regarded as one of the best hotels in the country, can cost around $225USD per night. If you don't mind spending around $125USD per night the Dann Carlton Hotel in Medellín is one of the most perfect hotels that we've ever stayed in and is a great value for the price.

↑ A typical Colombian menu showing food and prices

Itineraries

MEDELLÍN - A STARTING POINT

Since we're headquartered here, we thought that we would talk about it a little bit before moving onto the itineraries. We believe that Medellín is the best place in Colombia to start a motorcycle trip.

AIRPORT

Medellín has two airports but the one that you will fly into is a nice international airport called José María Córdova International Airport (MDE) which is located just outside of Medellín in a town called Rio Negro. The airport is relaxed and easy to navigate. It's not massive and chaotic like Bogotá with 30 million people traveling through. Getting to and from the airport is quick and easy and due to the opening of a new tunnel it now only takes 20-30 minutes to get from the airport to the El Poblado section of town, the part of Medellín that is most visited by travelers. Once you get off the plane the flow is pretty calm and straightforward. First thing, you go through immigration. Depending on what time you arrive there can be some pretty long lines in immigration but they usually aren't that bad. The people at immigration will ask to see your passport, where you will be staying, and

> If you want the best Caribbean beaches to go to the Bahamas, if you want the best Amazon go to Peru, if you want the most amazing Andes go to Peru, **but if you want them all in one place, go to Colombia.**

how long you will be here. Have the address of your hotel ready because they're going to be asking for it.

Next, pick up your suitcase and go through Customs. Here they may wave you through without inspecting your baggage or you may be subjected to a random inspection. The inspection is usually pretty quick and straightforward, and you are soon on your way.

Don't worry, they aren't trying to shake down foreigners and tax people for things in their suitcase.

Once you clear customs, it's time to find a taxi, and there will be no shortage of people asking you if you want to take a taxi. Blue and white taxis are airport taxis. You may wish to use these or call an UBER. If you're approached inside the terminal by a person trying to sell you a taxi ride, we advise you not to book with them and to instead go directly to the taxi stand just outside the doors and book your trip with them.

WEATHER

The City of Eternal Spring is a pretty self-explanatory nickname for Medellín. Medellín is the perfect and

Tandem paragliding flights are a popular activity in the hills outside of Medellín

↑ A striking sunset in Medellín

most livable Colombian destination and upon landing, you will find yourself in perfect springtime weather. Most days we wake up to nice cool mornings with temperatures around 17°C degrees (63°F) which rise to high temperatures around 27°C (82°F) in the afternoon before dropping back to cool temperatures again in the evening.

THINGS TO DO

Medellín is truly a cosmopolitan city with a million things to do. Everyone loves it here and the city is a fantastic travel destination with a wealth of fun activities.

PEOPLE-WATCHING IN PARQUE LLERAS - Medellín's premier nightlife hub is a brilliant spot for some people watching, especially on Thursday through Saturday nights when the city's hip young crowd hits the streets. Good food and even better clubbing attract locals and tourists alike, fusing into one huge partying scene that spills out of cool bars and clubs. The

> The mountains of Medellín make it the perfect place to go paragliding and get some stunning aerial views of the city.

↑ Heading off for a day trip

↑ Plaza Botero is a highlight during a trip to Medellín.

"park" in the name is a bit of a misnomer: this is essentially just two city blocks full of cafés, restaurants, bars, and people.

TAKE THE CABLE-CAR TO PARQUE ARVI - Parque Arvi is a large nature reserve on the north-eastern fringes of the city. Taking the cable car to the top makes a perfect half-day trip and gives you a birds-eye view of the city while flying over neighborhoods and taking in sweeping views of the valley below. Getting to Parque Arvi is pretty simple:

- Take the Metro train to the Acevedo station.

- Get off there and take the Santa Domingo cable car and ride it all the way to the top.

- Get off there and transfer to the Parque Arvi metrocable. This will take you the rest of the way to the park.

Essentially a collection of five distinct parks, Arvi boasts almost 150 species of exotic birds and butterflies and a lot of endemic flora. Open-air produce markets are the norm on weekends. With more than a dozen walking routes ranging between 1.5 and 4 hours, guided tours departing every half hour, a butterfly farm, zipline and so much more, Parque Arvi has enough to keep you busy for days on end. Make sure to bring some extra money as well as a jacket, or even a rain jacket, as it can get chilly and sometimes rain.

PARAGLIDING - The mountains of Medellín make it the perfect place to go paragliding and get some stunning aerial views of the city. Located just outside of Medellín and 10 minutes from our office, is the town of San Felix, known as the paragliding capital of Medellín.

TAKE A GUIDED TOUR OF COMUNA 13 - For decades, Comuna 13 was the kind of place not even the authorities could enter. The most dangerous hood in the most dangerous city in the world, however, has undergone one of the most spectacular transformations in all of Colombia and now offers fantastic guided tours to those who wish to see beyond

⬇ Riding through the backcountry outside of Medellín makes a great day trip.

the sparkly façade the city has tried hard to build. Brilliant street art and colorful characters are the primary reasons to visit this suburb. New infrastructure includes escalators and a brand-new cable car that has made life easier for locals. It has also literally opened up this fascinating place to outsiders.

> Riding through the backcountry outside of Medellín makes a great day trip.

↑ Taking the cable car to Parque Arvi makes a perfect half-day trip

PABLO ESCOBAR TOURISM - Given Narcos' extreme popularity, Escobar tourism has actually become pretty popular. You can visit his grave in the Jardíns Montesacro Cemetery in Itagui located in the south part of Medellín. You can also take guided tours of the most prominent Pablo-related places around Medellín. This kind of dark tourism is not exactly well-received in the country but there are a few tours that are heavy on the history without feeling like they're glorifying the most murderous drug-lord there was. Escobar was, at the end of the day, a pivotal character in Colombia's history and, when done well and with respect, these kinds of historical tours can be very insightful.

REAL CITY TOURS - Real City Tours offers walking tours of Medellín. The tours are free although you have to book in advance. The guides are excellent and explain the history of the country as well as the transformation of Medellín in a really good way. It's a very comprehensive and well-done walking tour and well well worth your time. You'll definitely want to tip the guide when the tour is done.

EAT BREAKFAST (OR DINNER) AT LAS HAMACAS OR LA VARIANTE - Located one block from our office, these two restaurants have authentic Colombian food at great prices, but the best part may be the views. Located on a hill outside of the city, the restaurants have panoramic views of Medellín and the entire Aburá Valley.

ABOUT OUR ITINERARIES

Starting in Medellín, since it's our base of operations, we organized the itineraries from nearest to farthest away. The itineraries and descriptions are not intended to be a complete list of every road in Colombia but rather a collection of places that are designed to give you a broad sampling of climates and communities in Colombia. The stops listed have a nice selection of hotels, restaurants, and services that are designed to make your trip easier and not put you into remote areas for your entire trip. The itineraries also give you the freedom to create your own adventure by leaving some of the more visited towns and go off-road to explore some of the smaller villages that offer the flavor of authentic Colombia.

DISTANCE - The distances between stops are listed but this can sometimes be misleading. Because of the

> These itineraries give you the freedom to leave some of the more visited towns and go off-road to explore some of the smaller villages that offer the flavor of authentic Colombia.

rough terrain, some days you cover 60km and it takes all day, other times you can do 60km in an hour. Also depending on your riding style, with stops for coffee, food, and admiring the views, most days are going to be pretty full.

HOTELS - We haven't had time to spend a night in each and every hotel in the region and give you a complete review of all of them. The hotels recommended below are clean and safe and we enjoyed staying there on our tours.

PEOPLE - The itineraries below mention some of the people that we met on our guided trips but don't think that it's impossible to meet people if you're traveling alone or don't speak the language. Being friendly and outgoing goes a long way. The Colombians are always happy to meet you and make new friends. All it takes is getting off the bike and saying hola!

JEFF & ALAN'S GUIDE TO MOTORCYCLE TRAVEL IN COLOMBIA

Day Trips From Medellín

The Milk Route

This the easiest of all of our day rides and completely paved. Traffic is minimal due to its rural location. Located in the hills outside of Medellín you'll be traveling up and away from the city congestion and won't have to bother with navigating your motorcycle through the maze of traffic in the city below. If you've just arrived in Colombia this is a great day trip to start things off.

The towns of San Felix, San Pedro, and Belmira are located on the Milk Route known as the "Ruta de Leche." Due to the rolling green hills and focus on dairy production the area is also known as the "Switzerland of Colombia." Located at high altitudes, the beautiful deep blue sky, thick green grass, and fresh cool air make it seem like you're riding through the Swiss Alps. The thick green pastures are located on both sides and filled with cows and you might get caught in a traffic jam of cows while a farmer is moving them between fields. You'll notice cowboys using donkeys to transport huge jugs of milk down the hillsides on their way to the market. Cowboys that aren't using donkeys have the jugs strapped to the back of small motorcycles. This is one of the experiences that make riding in the area special.

> This the easiest of all of our day rides. Traffic on this route is minimal due to its rural location. If you've just arrived in Colombia this is a great day trip to start things off.

Riding a motorcycle is the best way to experience a foreign country. Riding a motorcycle is the best way to experience a foreign country.

EL VOLADERO DE SAN FELIX - The San Felix Flying Area is your first stop on the milk route. The town of San Felix is also known as the paragliding capital of the region and you'll arrive in about 30 minutes. Here they use the mountain updrafts to soar high above the Andes and take in the views of the valley below. Even if you don't feel like paragliding it's still worth stopping and watching other people paragliding. There are a couple of restaurants overlooking the city where the paragliders pass so close you can actually hear them. The weather can get chilly up here so be sure to bring a sweatshirt and order the local favorite of hot chocolate with cheese.

SAN PEDRO - The next stop is San Pedro de Los Milagros via a beautifully paved road with green pastures and cattle ranches on both sides. Arriving

JEFF & ALAN'S GUIDE TO MOTORCYCLE TRAVEL IN COLOMBIA

↑ Coffee and Jungle Off-Road Loop-1 Cowboys using horses to transport huge jugs of milk to market. 84

↑ You might get caught in a traffic jam of horses and cows while the farmers move them between fields

in the small town you can make your way to the central square where there are several small restaurants. One is located on the second floor and offers you a perfect view of the square below and makes a good spot for a couple of photos.

The main attraction of the town is the "La Basílica Menor del Señor de Los Milagros de San Pedro" also known as the church. Even if you aren't into looking at churches it's still worth stopping in for a second to see the hand-painted ceiling.

LAKE LOOKOUT POINT - Located about 10 minutes outside of San Pedro heading towards the town of Entrerrios there is a viewpoint of a lake that makes for a nice photo opportunity.

BELMIRA - Belmira is an extremely small town where you can get a 100% authentic taste of Colombian cowboy culture. The ride to the town is absolutely beautiful. During the trip you are surrounded by green pastures and hills dotted with a fast-growing tropical species of tree with white leaves called White Cecropia (called Yarumo in Co-lombia). On the way, you can see farmers with mules bringing jugs of milk to the market. You might even get caught in the middle of a cattle drive since the farmers walk them on the road. Once arriving in the town you can check out the town square and the church and stop and get a coffee.

After leaving Belmira you can head straight back to Medellín via the same paved route that you came in on. The trip to this area just outside Medellín is one of our favorites.

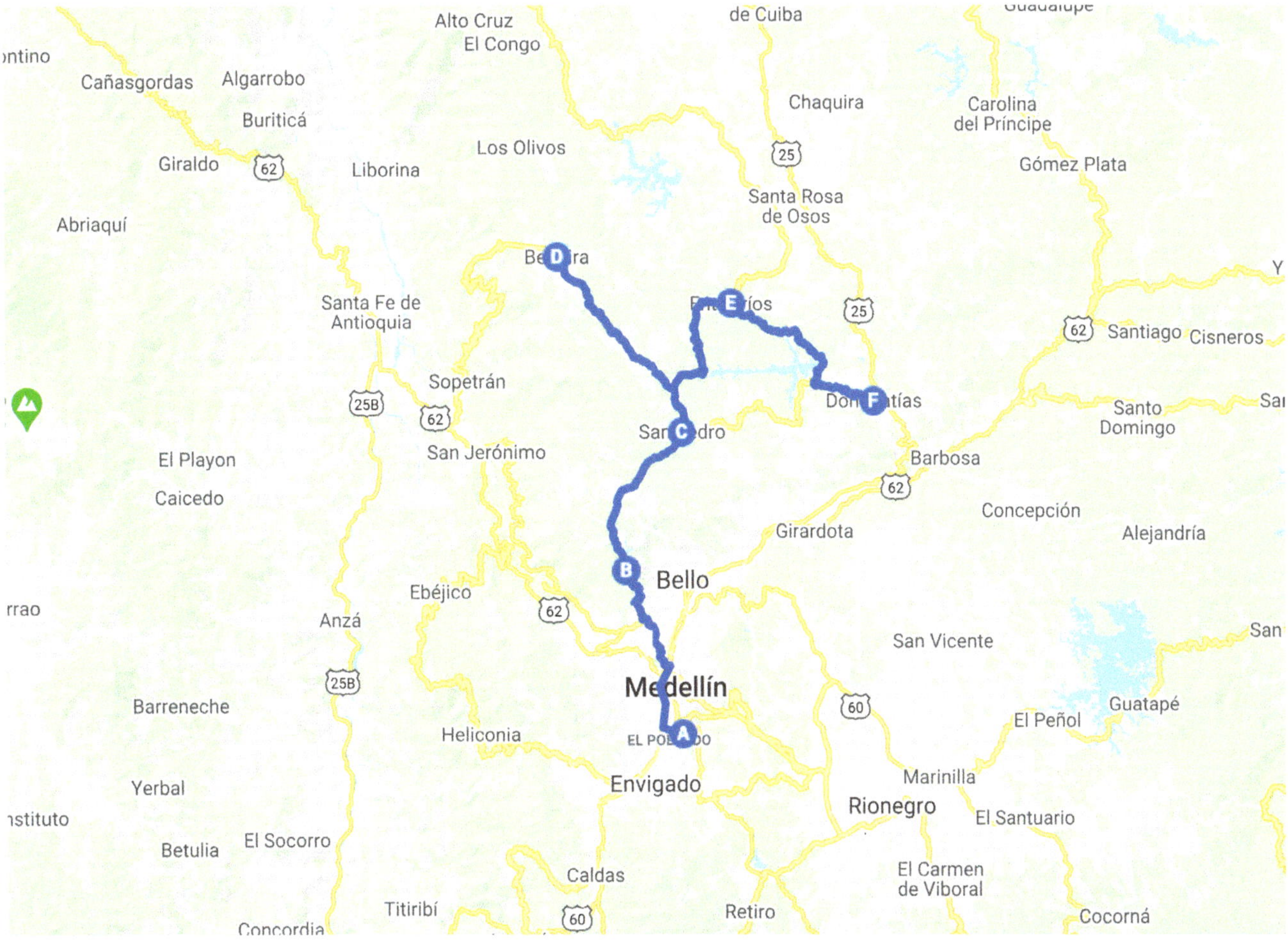

> Thick green pastures are located on both sides and filled with cows and you might get caught in a traffic jam of cows while a farmer is moving them between fields.

↑ Trout fishing is a popular activity outside of Medellín

Guatapé

The gorgeous town of Guatapé is a leisurely 1.5-hour ride from El Poblado (paved all the way) and makes for a fantastic 'lunch' outing and makes for a great intro to touring Colombia.

It's safe to say that pretty much all the towns in Colombia are beautiful and this one is no exception; the only difference is that here you can visit the famous Piedra del Peñol. This high granite monolith (technically an inselberg) rises from near the edge of a man-made lake, the Embalse Guatapé. A brick staircase of 659 steps rises up through a broad fissure on the side of the rock. From the top, you'll soak up magnificent views of this fertile region, the fingers of the lake sprawling amid a vast expanse of green mountains.

After coming down, find a spot in the restaurant below, that boasts a view of the lake. Order up a huge bandeja paisa complete with beans, rice, chorizo and avocado, and of course a cold beer or guanabana juice.

Some tourist attractions are just too good to ignore!

Recommended Hotel:
Hotel Zocalo Campestre or Hotel Mansion Guatapé

Recommended Boutique Hotel:
Bosko Luxury Glamping

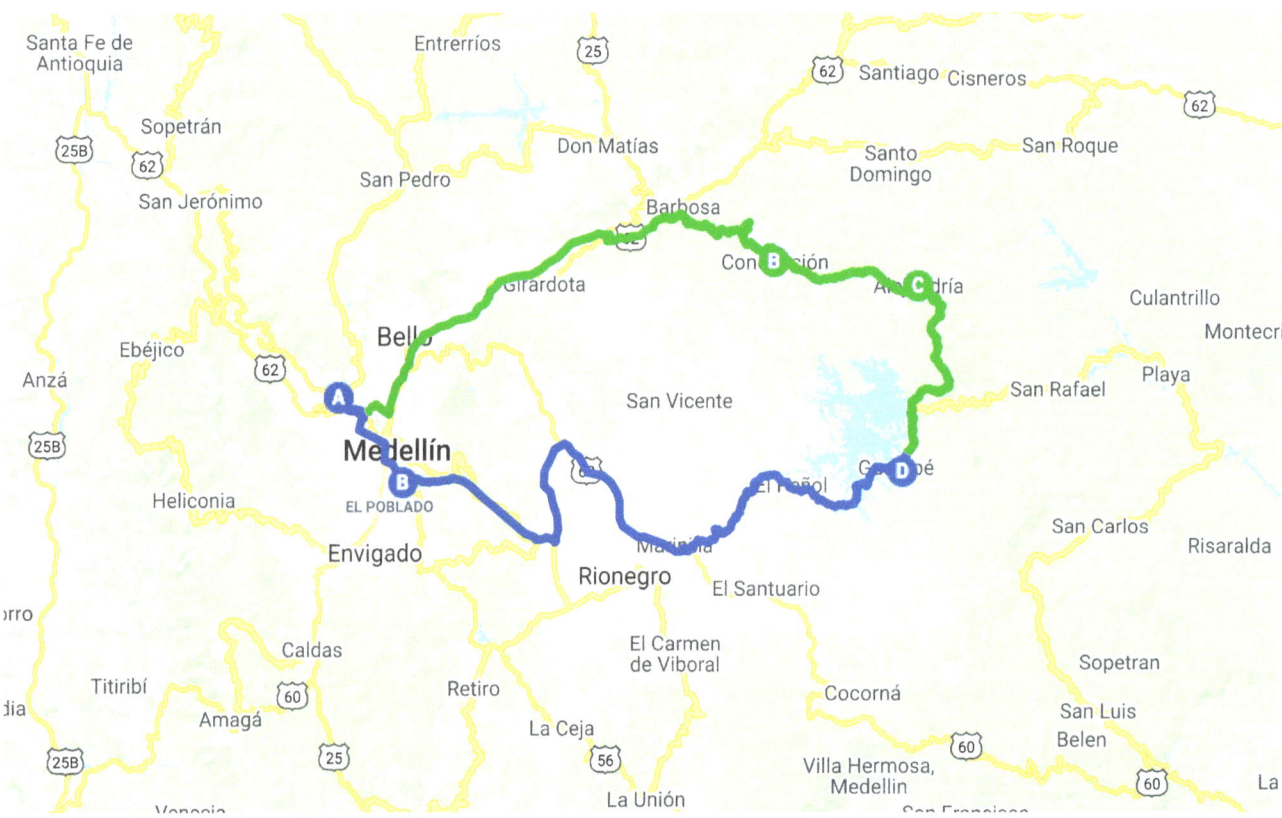
↑ There are two ways to get to Guatapé. The blue route is paved and the green route is more off-road oriented.

↑ A ride to Guatapé makes a great day trip.

↑ Guatapé is a lovely little lakeside town less than two hours from Medellín

↑ The number one reason for visiting Guatapé is to climb the 740 steps to the top of the El Peñón de Guatapé ("The Rock of Guatapé")

Cocorna is a great place to get lunch and watch paragliders fly by your table as well as circle around a nearby waterfall

Cocorná

Cocorná is a small town located two hours from Medellín. The town is a popular place for watersports due to its many waterfalls, swimming holes, and river tubing locations. Its warm tropical climate makes it the perfect place to take a break from the cooler climates of Medellín and spend a day swimming.

The trip to Cocorná is short and there are a couple of nice stops along the way. We recommend making your first stop at the Segundo Mirador De Las Palmas or Second Las Palmas Lookout Point. Located only a few minutes outside the city on your route, the lookout point offers a spectacular view across Medellín and the Aburrá Valley. If you want to grab a coffee or empanadas before heading out we recommend stopping at the Estadero El Zarzal located just a little further up the road. The route is easy and Google Maps will get you there, and all the other spots, with no trouble.

The rest of the trip takes you down the highway while passing through some of the more populated outlying towns of Rio Negro, Guarne, and Marinilla before hitting the more rural areas closer to Cocorná. There are a couple of toll booths along the way but motorcycles don't need to pay and can pass the toll using a small lane located to the right of the toll booth. The route from Medellín to Cocorná is located on the Medellín - Bogotá highway so there will be traffic on the route until you reach Cocorná.

Located on a ridge before arriving into Cocorná the Restaurante Ktarata restaurant offers amazing views of the valley and great food. You can also watch paragliders fly by your table as they circle around a nearby waterfall. The paragliding company is conveniently located next door to the restaurant. If you decide to fly we recommend eating lunch after the flight.

Local swimming holes, called charcos, make great places to swim. Balneario El Descanso is one of the more popular spots and is located a few minutes past the restaurant. This swimming zone is easily accessible and has a small restaurant nearby. If you're looking for a place with fewer people we recommend heading past the village of Vereda La Piñuela and checking out the numerous swimming spots located along the Río Melcocho.

JEFF & ALAN'S GUIDE TO MOTORCYCLE TRAVEL IN COLOMBIA

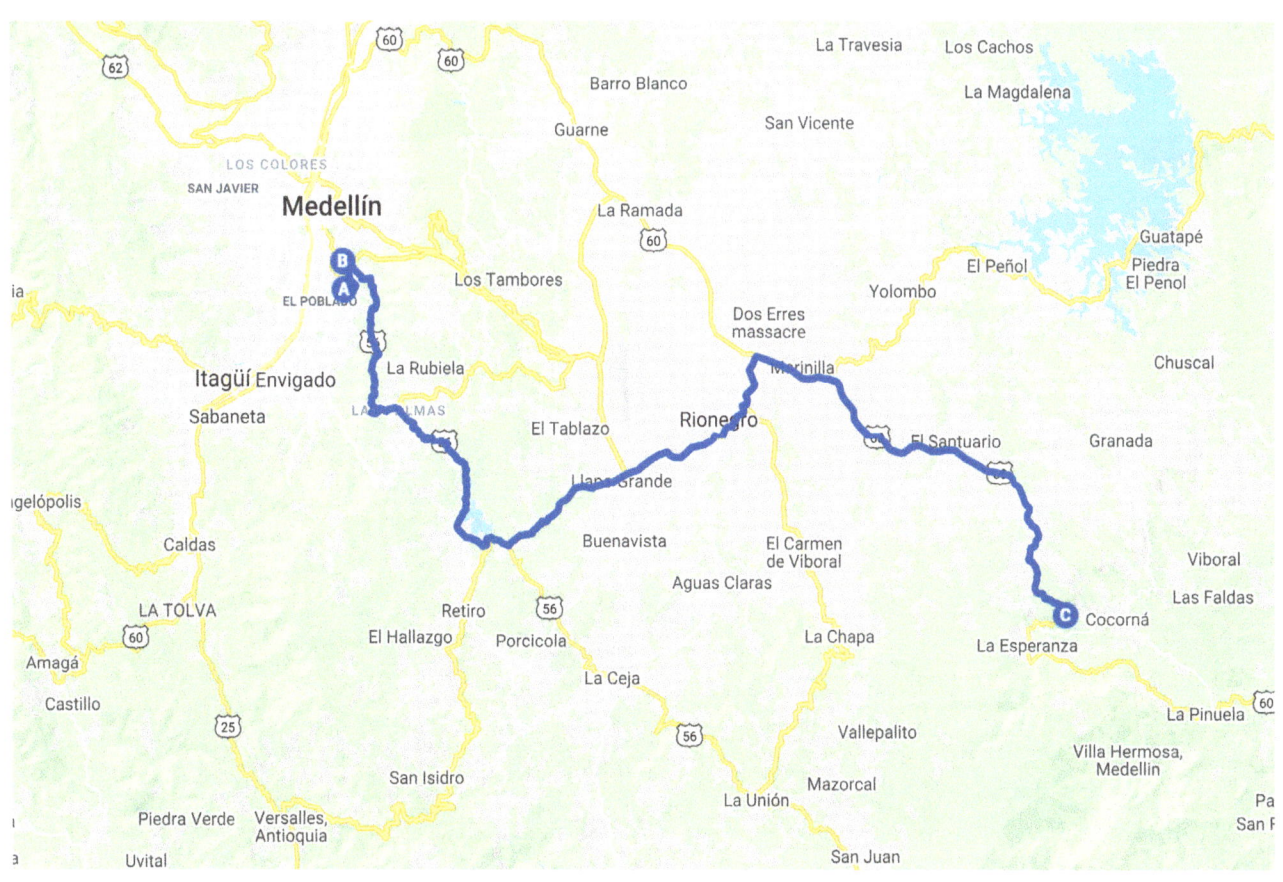

ColombiaMotoAdventures.com

JEFF & ALAN'S GUIDE TO MOTORCYCLE TRAVEL IN COLOMBIA

Overnight Trips

↑ Loading your motorcycle into a dugout canoe makes for a great story!

San Carlos

San Carlos is a small town that hasn't yet been discovered by many foreigners. Having been off-limits for years due to guerrila violence in the area and only within the past few years has the town opened up for foreigners to explore. About a four hours ride from Medellín, the ride to San Carlos takes you through winding mountains, rivers, and waterfalls before dropping you down into a tropical valley. San Carlos is known for its variety of nature activities including hiking, waterfalls, and swimming in the nearby rivers. The food is cheap, the coffee is great, and unlike Guatapé, you won't need a jacket at night.

HIGHLIGHTS

- Waterfalls in San Carlos
- Snaking through mountain roads
- Beautiful scenery the entire time
- Steak dinner on the town square
- Guatapé
- El Peñol Rock

DAY 1 — Medellín To San Carlos

The motorcycle trip to San Carlos takes you through a winding road passing through the town of Granada. The road is totally beautiful with spectacular views. Sometimes there is mountain mist which makes the scenery even more magical.

Once you get to San Carlos, we recommend taking a hike to the 30 meter tall La Viejita waterfall. La Viejita is a nature trail of approximately one mile (900 meters) with easy access and is one of the most beautiful trails in the area. Climbing up further along the trail, you come to a second waterfall known as "La Cascada" that has a pool of water at the bottom for swimming. If you want to explore other waterfalls and swimming holes we recommend getting a local guide. You can check with the local tourism office, called SENA, located in the town square to find reputable guides.

Recommended Hotel:
Hotel Campestre La Cascada

Located walking distance from the Hotel Campestre La Cascada is the San Antonio waterfall. The path has a couple of covered bridges that cross a stream and the paved trail is covered by trees and surrounded by nature. The hike and seeing the waterfall makes for good photo opportunities but they aren't exactly the best for swimming due to the rushing water flowing through.

A short motorcycle ride out to the other side of San Carlos is the huge Piedra del Tabor that dominates the landscape. This gigantic Stone Monolith rises to a height of about 9,500 feet (1,800 meters) above sea level. It is possible to climb to the top but it takes around 8 hours round trip and there is thick vegetation.

Steak dinner on the town square is a great evening activity. We recommend checking out the Al Carbón de Leña restaurant that has great steak. La Costica Dulce restaurant is also recommended and has a great view of the town square from the second floor.

JEFF & ALAN'S GUIDE TO MOTORCYCLE TRAVEL IN COLOMBIA

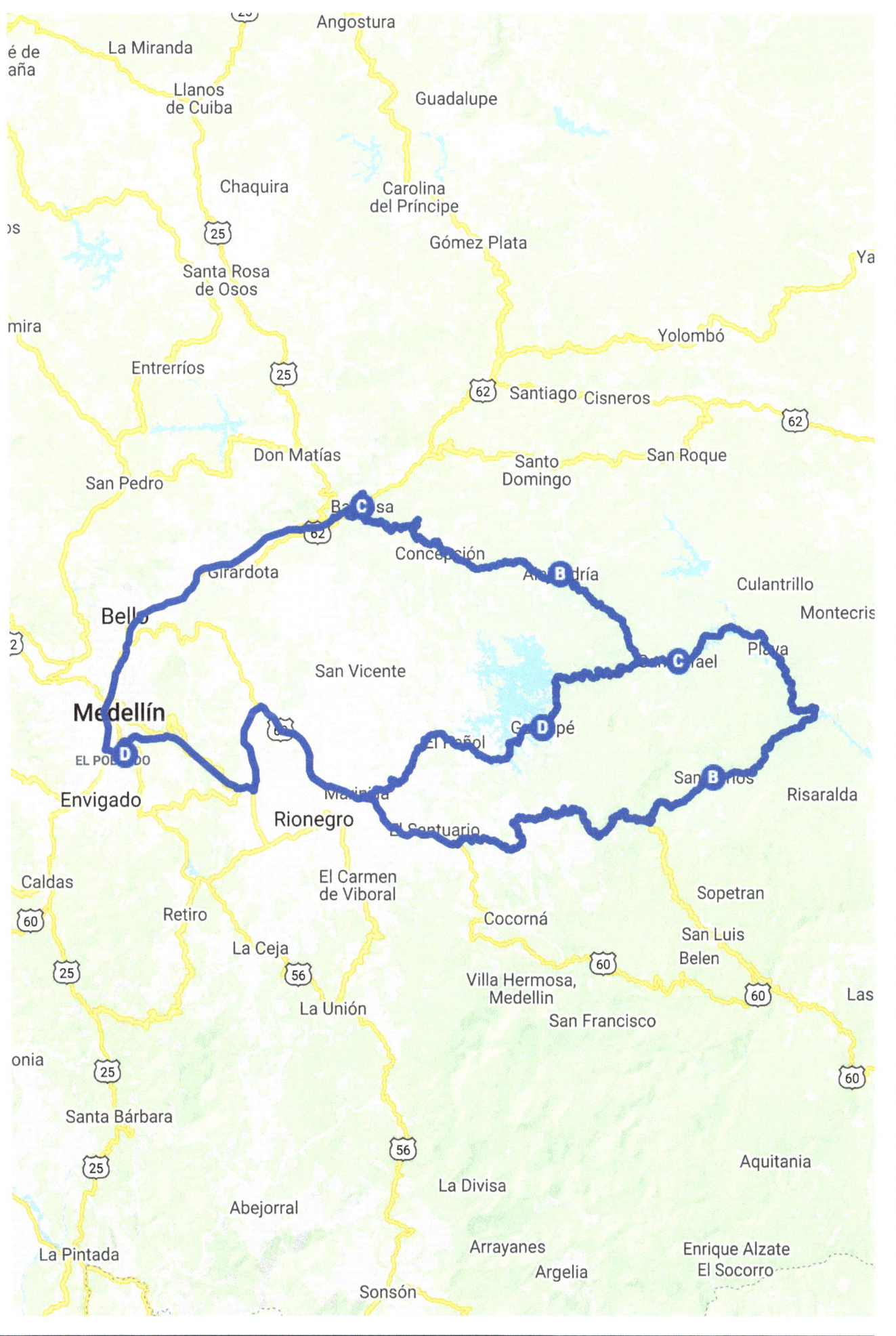

DAY 2 — San Carlos To Guatapé Then Back To Medellín

Day two is another great day and the ride to Guatapé is beautiful. Leaving San Carlos, head north past the Mirador San Carlos lookout point towards San Rafael. This road is rugged and unpaved and starts off taking you across the top of a mountain. Dropping down from the mountain, you will ride off-road through a valley before arriving in the town of San Rafael. San Rafael is a convenient place to stop and get a quick cup of coffee before riding the final 45 minutes to Guatapé on pavement.

The big draw here is the famous Piedra del Peñol and the view of the lake and surrounding area from the top. The Piedra is a high granite monolith (technically an inselberg) that rises from near the edge of a man-made lake called the Embalse Guatapé. A brick staircase of 659 steps rises up through a broad fissure on the side of the rock. From the top, you'll soak up magnificent views of this fertile region, the fingers of the lake sprawling amid a vast expanse of green mountains.

Guatapé is a nice town but can be quite touristy and crowded, especially on weekends and holidays. There are shops selling t-shirts, wood carvings, and other souvenirs on pretty much every corner. That being said, it's still worth it to visit and some tourist attractions are just too good to pass up.

The ride to Medellín takes around two hours on a paved road and is fairly uneventful if there isn't any traffic. Starting about an hour after leaving Guatapé you will notice that the traffic begins to get heavier. Highway congestion from busses and people returning to Medellín can make the highway more challenging. The last leg of the trip dropping into Medellín's valley is a bit steeper so be sure to watch your speed and increase your following distance.

↑ Colombias paved roads make it easy to ride 2-up

San Carlos is filled with rivers and waterfalls and makes a great overnight trip from Medellín

Jardin

Jardin makes for a perfect overnight trip. It's going to give you a nice taste of your first longer ride in Colombia and will take you through a couple of different climate zones on your way to the town. The ride isn't demanding or technical and is all paved. Coming down out of the mountains of Medellín you cross the Cauca river valley. Be prepared for the temperature to rise as the valleys are hot and the terrain becomes semi-desert. After the arid parts, the curves increase as you wind your way back into the lush green mountains.

Revered for its brightly-colored houses and quaint mountainside location, Jardín is often dubbed 'the most beautiful town in all of Colombia. In town, you can simply stroll the little colonial streets, admire the stunning architecture, and be enticed by a charming coffee house - the center is compact and easily explored on foot. The area also has a large selection of hotels ranging from low-cost hostels to upscale boutique hotels that are definitely up to western standards.

 Recommended Hotel:
Lulo's Hostal

Recommended Boutique Hotel:
Casa Passiflora Hotel Boutique

CABLE CARS - A great way to get a bird's eye view of the town is by cablecar. La Garucha is a home built metal lattice cable car that pulls you across a valley while suspended hundreds of meters in the air. The views of the city, mountains, and valley below are incredible and there is a restaurant located on the other side.

LA CUEVA DEL ESPLENDOR - A hidden highlight of Jardín is found just outside the town, though: a magnificent spot called the Cave of Splendor (La Cueva del Esplendor). The best way to see this splendor is on a 12-mile hike, which is hard work but rewarding - you'll come face to face with a spectacular cave that has a waterfall cascading right through its roof. You can enjoy a refreshing swim here so pack your swimmers. The cave is on private property and there's a small charge to enter.

COLORFUL BIRDS - Visiting the Parque Natural Jardín de Rocas is a must-do trip for birdwatchers. You can see the shockingly bright orange and black Gallo de Roca Andino also known as the Andean Cock-Of-The-Rock. Located at what is known as a lek, we can see courtship displays with males trying to impress the females. The best time to go is in the early morning and just before dusk. You can get within feet of the birds as they socialize to start and end their days.

Although undeniably beautiful, Jardín has become a tad touristy in recent years and if you're looking to avoid the crowds, you may actually have a more enjoyable time in the nearby town of Jericó instead.

Jardin is the best place to see the brilliant red-orange Andean Cock-of-the-rock

JEFF & ALAN'S GUIDE TO MOTORCYCLE TRAVEL IN COLOMBIA

↑ Jardin is often dubbed "the most beautiful town in all of Colombia"

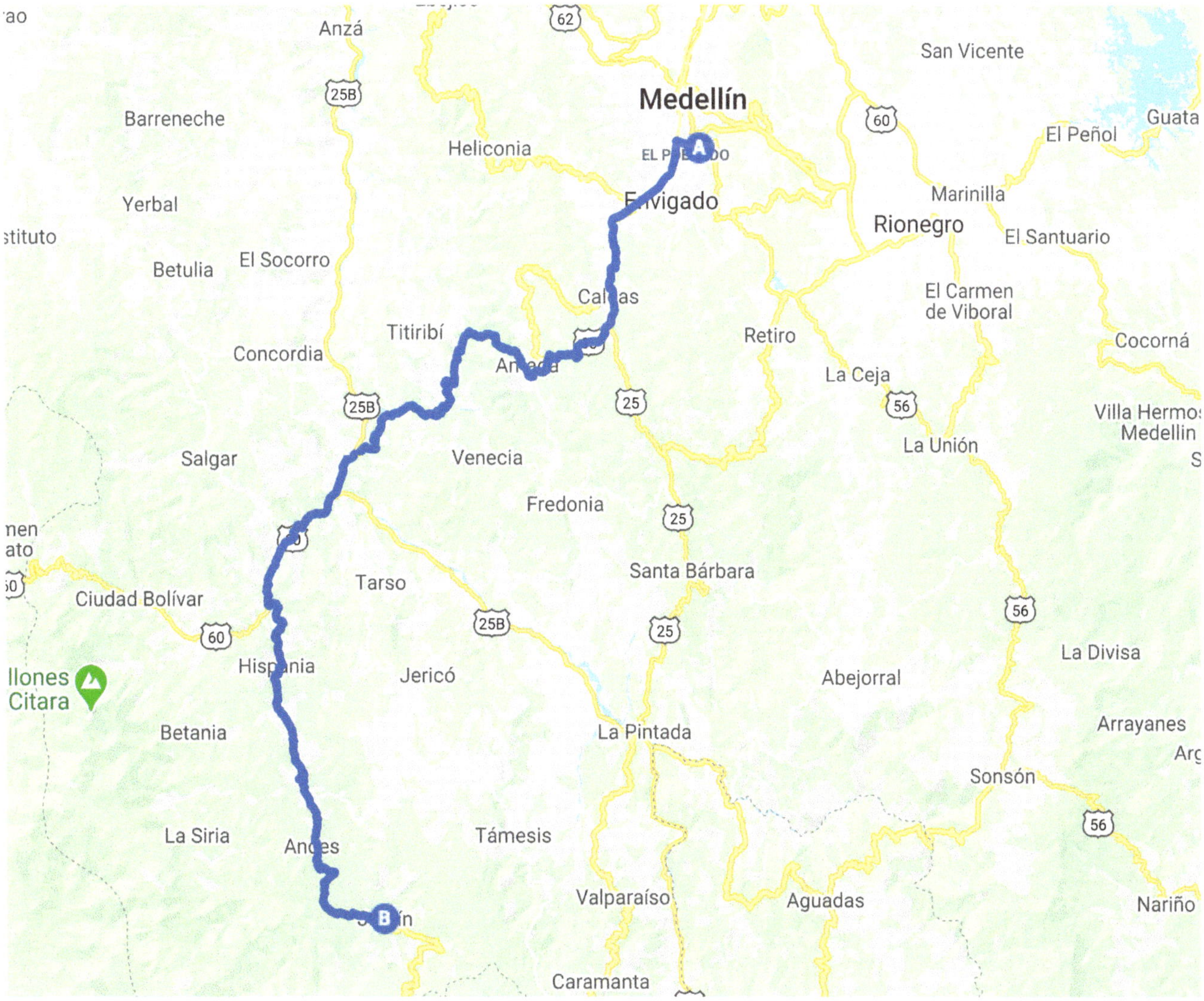

Jerico

Guatapé and Jardín tend to dominate the lists of day trips, but Jericó is equally beautiful and interesting, minus the tourist crowds, and getting there is half the fun.

Much like Jardín, Jericó boasts wonderful colonial architecture in its historic core and offers fantastic nature-based activities in its surrounding mountainous landscapes. Hiking and paragliding here are phenomenal and this is, undoubtedly, the paragliding capital of Colombia and the active-pursuits attract a small but dedicated group of adventure-mad travelers, both local and international.

Getting to Jericó is half the fun with the final selection of roads being amazing to ride. Starting from Medellín you head south towards the town of Bolombolo where you cross the Cauca River. Following the signs to Jericó, the road begins to climb uphill with dozens of hairpin curves revealing vast views of the jungle valley below. There are a couple of small authentic restaurants built into the side of the mountain dishing up great local food and equally great panoramic views. Grabbing a coffee or some empanadas here is the perfect place to break up the trip before arriving in town.

Coffee tours are also huge in Jericó and you can visit a working finca and learn all about the processing of this incredible bean. There's a farm perched atop a steep canyon overlooking the Cauca River, the second-longest in Colombia, right above a striking waterfall - this is one of the most jaw-dropping settings of any farm you'll find in the country, so don't miss it! A tour to this family-owned farm is run by the guys and gals at Las Cometas Hostel.

And don't forget that paragliding is also on offer in Jericó - most tours take flight from the Puerto Arturo viewpoint. Pick a crystal-clear morning and enjoy the breathtaking pyramid mountain of Cerro Tusa.

Jericó is a Pueblo Patrimonio (preserved towns) and easily reached within 3 hours riding from Medellín. Although a day-trip is possible, staying overnight makes for a better excursion.

> Recommended Hotel:
> **Las Cometas Hostel**

Guatapé and Jardin tend to dominate the lists of day trips, but Jericó is equally beautiful and interesting

JEFF & ALAN'S GUIDE TO MOTORCYCLE TRAVEL IN COLOMBIA

↑ Dozens of hairpin curves revealing vast views of the jungle valley below.

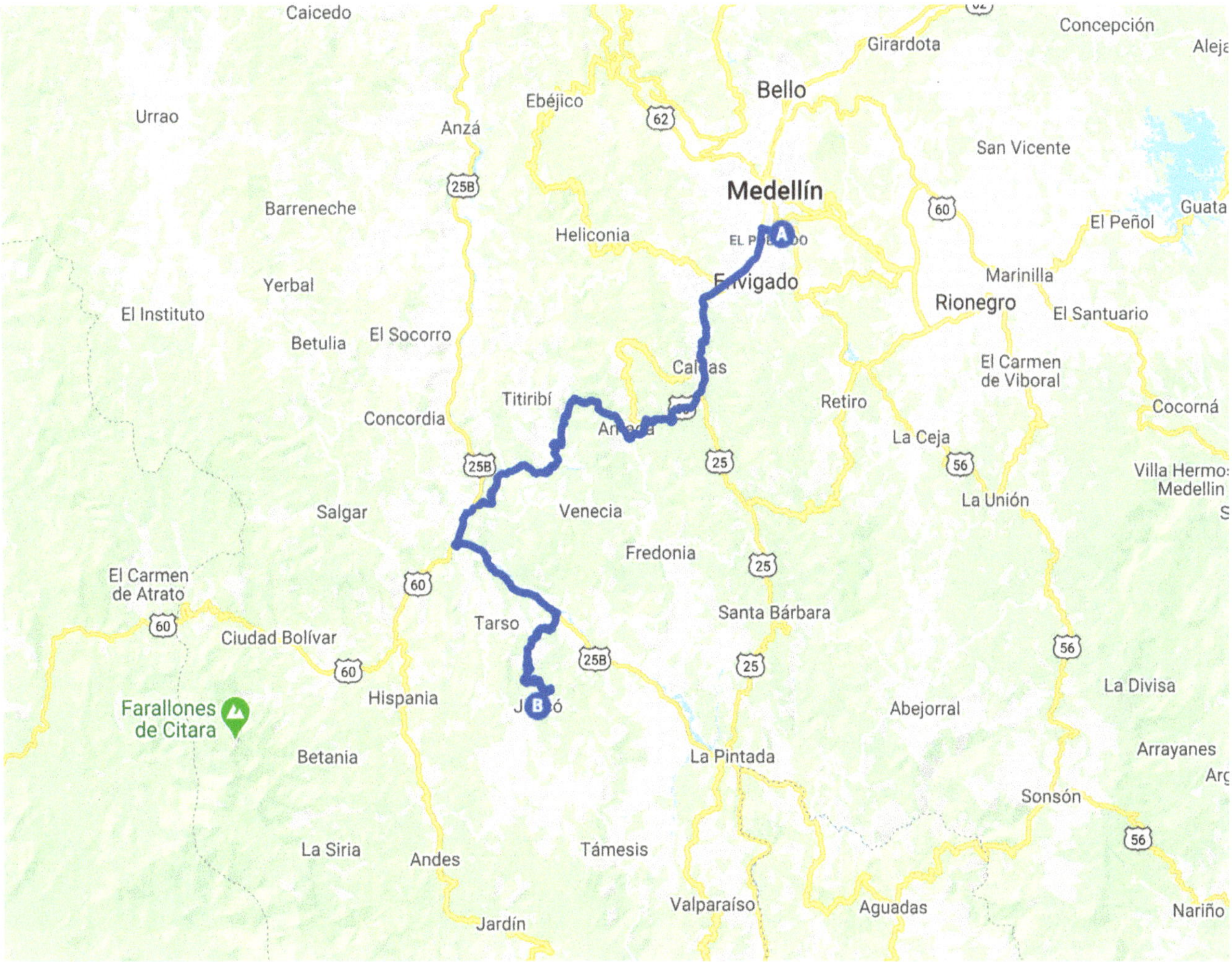

One Week Trips

↑ Perched on a mountain top, Salamina is an undiscovered gem in the north of Caldas department

JEFF & ALAN'S GUIDE TO MOTORCYCLE TRAVEL IN COLOMBIA

Windows of Tisquizoque

ITINERARY

DAY 1
MEDELLÍN TO LANDÁZURI

Leave Medellín we wind our way through the mountains outside of the city. The road is paved the entire way and features gentle sweeping curves that are easy to handle. This is an easy way to begin the trip and get used to driving in Colombia. Once we drop into the tropical Magdalena valley the terrain becomes flat for the next few hours. Towering in the distance we begin to close in on a totally new mountain range, the rugged Eastern Andes.

Here we begin to enter a tropical cloud forest where the temperature begins to cool off and is a welcome change compared to earlier in the day. Spending the night in the small town of Landázuri we can grab a bite to eat in the town square and prepare for the next day's ride.

DAY 2
LANDÁZURI TO FLORIÁN

Get ready for some rugged high-altitude riding. We are going to spend the entire day in the backcountry where the inhabitants rarely come into contact with foreigners. We'll repeatedly climb and descend through jagged mountains and valleys caused by a series of folded tectonic fault lines. Guaranteed that you've never seen anything like this. Panoramic views are around every corner, and cold mist rolling through the landscape adds a "Lord of the Rings" dimension to the ride. Although the topography is rough, the roads are in surprisingly good shape consisting of well maintained hard-packed gravel.

We'll finish our journey on a road that snakes through a narrow canyon. Surrounded by steep rock walls on both sides we follow a winding river for miles before reaching our final destination, the town of Florián. The entire ride takes around five hours although stopping for photographs, coffee and food will turn it into an all-day ride.

DAY 3
WINDOWS OF TISQUIZOQUE

Florian is home to the Windows of Tisquizoque, a remote and rarely visited three-tiered waterfall that plummets from a mountain cave with fantastic views over the countryside. We spend the day exploring the enormous cave located almost 1000ft above the valley floor. Here we will stand at the edge of the dropoff and take pictures of nearby towns and surrounding mountains. Afterward, we will ride down and swim

↑ Windows of Tisquizoque is the perfect place to get cinematic photos from a drone

Visiting this amazing place feels like going into a Jurassic Park movie

in the plunge pool at the base of the waterfall.

Sealed off for decades due to its remote location and past guerrilla activity Florián is a town that hasn't yet been developed for tourism. Florián still feels new and authentic and you'll be glad you visited before it becomes spoiled by mass tourism. Visiting the town square, talking to the locals, and eating home-cooked meals made by the restaurant owners give us a unique insight into small-town life in Colombia.

DAY 4
FLORIÁN TO LAS GACHAS

Today we are leaving Florián, heading to another beautiful and rarely visited place, Quebrada Las Gachas. The ride today is almost exclusively pavement and takes us through a high valley. We make a few stops along the way to rest and get snacks but the main mission today is to arrive at Las Gachas.

Popular with locals but still unknown to foreigners, Las Gachas is a series of natural "jacuzzi-like" pools along a shallow river bed. Your friends won't believe you when you tell them about this place. There are over a hundred pools along the creek where you can slide, swim, and immerse yourself in the pools. Some of the pools are small and only fit one person, while others are larger and can hold more than five people. The area is sometimes called the "rainbow river" since the color of the water appears to be red and green. These colors are due to the rocks and minerals in the river. There is an easy 10 to 15-minute walk to get there, but it's worth the effort, and the views are gorgeous.

After spending the afternoon swimming we overnight in the nearby town of Guadalupe. Guadalupe is a town surrounded by mountains and hills in every direction, giant palm trees in the square. It's a small town and there are just a few shops and restaurants to choose from but the peacefulness is a welcome contrast to the busy city life of Medellín.

DAY 5
LAS GACHAS TO LANDÁZURI

Taking a different route, we head back to Landázuri through the remote tropical highlands. This ride is all off-road and has us climbing and winding our way through mountainous switchbacks. The day is full of major elevation changes and gorgeous views. The area is so remote that the places barely show up on google maps! This trip is a great way to see authentic Colombia, where tourists have never been. The drive takes us through tiny villages where we can stop and get coffee and lunch. The locals are a curious bunch and are interested in people visiting their towns. If you're brave and attempt to start up a conversation you'll be surprised at how friendly they are.

DAY 6
LANDÁZURI TO MEDELLÍN

Back to the City of Eternal Spring. In the morning we drop back down from the mountain ranges and cross the plains of Colombia. In the afternoon, we twist back up into the mountains and end the trip back at our headquarters in beautiful Medellín. The route is the same that we took on day one but as Confucius says "A motorcyclist doesn't know a road until he's ridden it in both directions."

↑ The huge plunge pool is the perfect place to swim after exploring the cave and waterfall

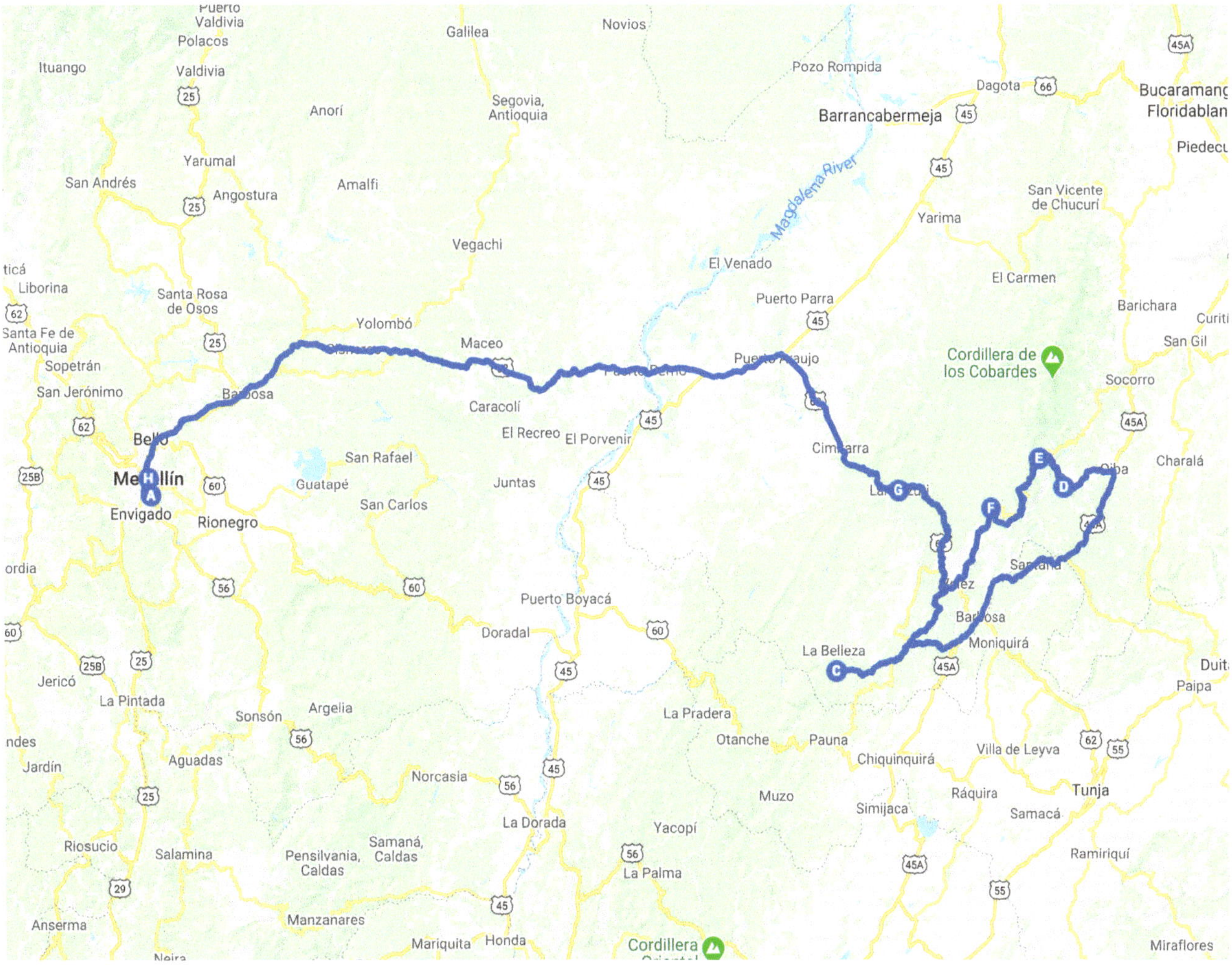

JEFF & ALAN'S GUIDE TO MOTORCYCLE TRAVEL IN COLOMBIA

JEFF & ALAN'S GUIDE TO MOTORCYCLE TRAVEL IN COLOMBIA

The Perfect Loop:
Exploring The Coffee Region

↑ Over 2 million Colombians depend on coffee production for income

Colombia's best geography for coffee production also happens to be ideal for motorcycle riding. If you're looking to experience the best of Colombia and only have a week, we highly recommend this trip. Based on the feedback from dozens of travelers, we have put together what we consider to be the "Perfect Loop" of Colombia's famous coffee region. Best of all, it's located right in our backyard, only 2 hours from Medellín.

The coffee region checks all the boxes: Lush green mountain vistas with soaring wax palms over 150ft tall. Check. Colonial haciendas turned into chic hotels and bed and breakfasts. Check. Hot springs flowing from snow-capped volcanoes. Check. Twist the throttle and lean into turn after turn after turn as you make your way through high mountain passes and fog covered forests. Check. Include the cosmopolitan city of Medellín as the starting point of the trip, and you have a motorcycle trip from heaven.

HIGHLIGHTS

- **Guatapé -** Climb the Piedra de Peñol in Guatapé

- **Nevado del Ruiz Volcano -** Explore a stratovolcano

- **Thermal Springs -** Stay at a hot springs hotel in Manizales

- **Wax Palms -** Visit The Wax Palm Forest

- **Spectacular Views -** As always, enjoying all the twists and turns while riding through some of the amazing scenery in the world.

DAY 1 — Medellín - Guatapé

The trip to Guatapé is short, and there are a couple of nice stops along the way. We recommend making your first stop at the Segundo Mirador De Las Palmas or Second Las Palmas Lookout Point. Located only a few minutes outside the city on our route, the lookout point offers a spectacular view across Medellín. If you want to grab a coffee or empanadas before heading out, we recommend stopping at the Estadero El Zarzal located just a little further up the road. The route is easy, and Google Maps will get you there and all the other spots, with no trouble.

The big draw in Guatapé is climbing

Recommended Hotel:
Hotel Zocalo Campestre or Hotel Mansion Guatapé

Recommended Boutique Hotel:
Bosko Luxury Glamping

the famous Piedra del Peñol. The Piedra is a high granite monolith (technically an inselberg) that rises from near the edge of a man-made lake called the Embalse Guatapé. A brick staircase of 659 steps rises up through a broad fissure on the side of the rock. From the top, we'll soak up magnificent views of the region, the fingers of the lake sprawling amid a vast expanse of green mountains.

After your climb of "El Peñon de Guatapé," you can walk the streets of the town, snapping photos of the brightly colored houses. Here, you'll have the chance to dine on fresh empanadas and drink ice cold cerveza michelada.

Guatapé is a nice town but can be quite touristy and crowded, especially on weekends and holidays. There are shops selling t-shirts, wood carvings, and other souvenirs on pretty much every corner. That being said, a visit to Guatapé is still worth it, and some tourist attractions are just too good to pass up.

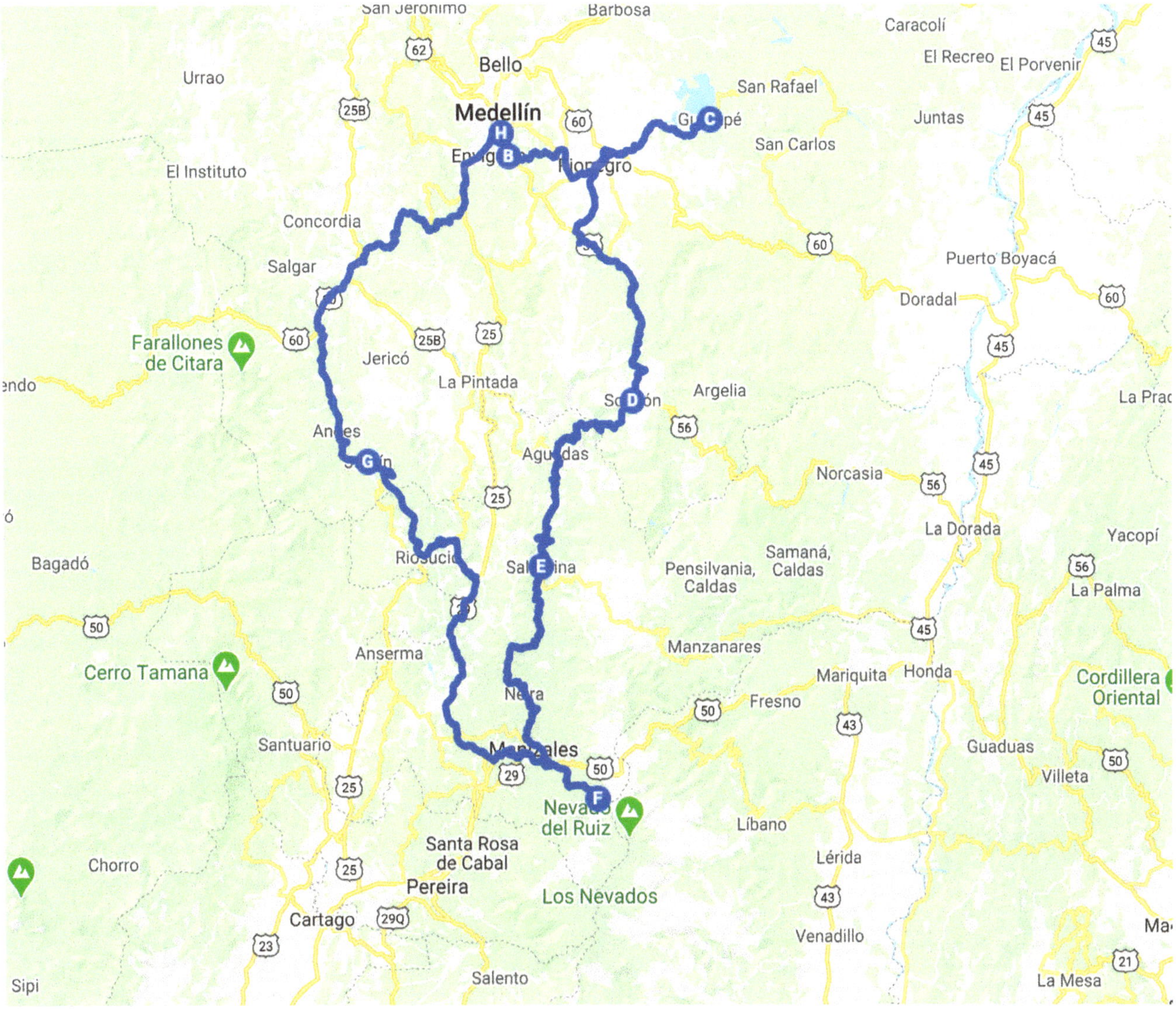

DAY 2 Guatapé – Sonsón

Today we ride to the former guerilla conflict zone of Sonsón. Sonsón has a rich history and was one of the founding towns of Colombia's famous coffee axis. It has been off-limits for decades due to guerilla activity. Although it's safe now there is very little information on the internet about the area. Consequently, it's untouched by tourism which makes it the perfect place to get an authentic taste of Colombia.

The ride to Sonsón is great. One of the best things about this ride is the miles and miles of exciting twists and turns. Ups, downs, ascending curves, descending curves, increasing radius curves, decreasing radius curves. You're going to get a ton of riding experience on just this one road. The pavement here is in good shape and as is the case in lots of areas in the countryside, there is very little traffic.

Midway we're going to stop off at Luisa's house and have a cup of local coffee called tinto. If you like kids you'll be delighted to meet her twin toddlers. Tourists never stop here and you'll see how happy she is to talk with us. Besides being a fun way to connect with the locals, it's a way to directly support a family business.

We'll visit the HALO demining opera-

 Recommended Hotel:
Hotel: El Tesoro

tions and learn about their efforts to remove leftover anti-personnel landmines from the area. We get the chance to hold deactivated landmines they have recovered. Yep, there are still landmines out here.

The town of Sonsón is located at a high elevation but we're going to climb even higher. The Páramo de Sonsón is a lookout point that stands at over 10,000ft in elevation. The lookout has a scenic view of the fog rolling across the cloud forest and nearby valley. By now it will be late afternoon and we'll head back to town to check in to our hotel and grab a pizza and a beer.

We stay at the El Tesoro hotel located on the main square. This is a 215-year-old hacienda (former rural homestead) that has been converted into a unique hotel. Unlike other hotels, this one hasn't been updated and still retains its original charm.

The interior of the hotel is designed using "Andalusian patios." This style of architecture, imported from Mediterranean Spain, uses a series of rectangular courtyards surrounded by covered balconies to shield people from the sun and rain. The hotel is constructed using a combination of rammed earth on the lower floor and a special type of lightweight and earthquake-resistant construction called "Bahareque" on the second floor. Bahreque, also called "Quincha" in Peru, is a traditional way of building in which wooden frames or panels support a mesh of sugarcane stalks to which are then finished with a plaster of mud, gypsum, and straw.

During the founding of the coffee region, the hacienda had a lot of different uses. It was first used as a place to store local crops of coffee, corn, and beans which are grown in the cold climate. Later on, the hotel was used to hold parties and gatherings of local landowners and was frequented by many presidents and governors of Colombia before being turned into the hotel today.

One of the most interesting things about the hotel is its eclectic collection of antiques. Over the years the current owners have amassed a collection of some really interesting items including a rope driven dental drill and chair, huge wrenches, old coins as well as 910 keys. Looking over everything will keep you captivated for hours.

Located next door to the hotel is a great pizza restaurant. From the second-story balcony, we can enjoy a brick oven pizza while people-watching on the main square. Sonsón leaves the warm weather of Guatapé behind. Located at 8,100ft you'll want to bring a jacket because it's going to be cold at night.

Solar drying of coffee is used by 90% of Colombian coffee producers

DAY 3 — Sonsón to Salamina

Salamina is Colombia's best-kept secret. Tucked away in a far off corner of the coffee region, the beauty of Salamina is a sight to behold. The town itself is situated on the peak of a mountain, with entire streets sometimes appearing as if they are about to slide off the side of the mountain. Once we enter the town, we see why it has earned national heritage status. Houses climb the sloping streets with each one determined to outdo its neighbors. Elaborate woodworking takes the form of intricately decorated doors, windows, balconies, and zócalos (the distinct lower sections of the whitewashed facades). It's hard to walk the streets of Salamina without constantly looking upward at the flower-filled balconies.

A gorgeous bronze basin fountain made in Paris sits in the central plaza surrounded by tall trees and benches. In 1900 the fountain was brought to town on the back of ox and mules and since then it has become a symbol of the region. There are also various restaurants surrounding the main square where you can try typical local dishes, including the local favorite of steamed eggs (Huevos al Vapor), which is made with the help of an espresso machine.

The road from Sonsón is unpaved but in good condition. Almost as soon as we leave Sonsón we have to stop to take photos of the expansive valley right outside of town. The rest of the ride consists of windy roads and spectacular views of the surrounding coffee and sugarcane plantations. In the middle of the trip, we drop into a warm valley and cross a bridge over a white water river before snaking back into the mountains on the other side. Just before we arrive in town, there's a panoramic view of the town precariously sitting on the top of a hill.

One of the nicer boutique options in Salamina is the Casa de Lola Garcia. Formerly a coffee hacienda, the owners have beautifully restored the house and converted it into a charming boutique hotel. The property is complete with spacious rooms, king-sized beds, and a beautiful courtyard with jasmine trees and a jacuzzi. The hotel has a perfect location and is only a two-minute walk from the main square.

Optional Route - Instead of heading directly to Salamina today, you can add a day to the trip and drive from Sonsón down into the jungle, past Norcasia. Have lunch or stay at the quaint hot-springs hotel (Espiritu Santo) where rooms are simple and the springs lovely - the restaurant is decent here and the river is great. From there, take the backroads across the mountains to the isolated villages of Pensilvania (yep, that's the correct spelling) or Samaná located in the department of Caldas. After spending the night, you can take a rarely traveled road through Manzanares to Marulanda and then onto Salamina. One of the most beautiful roads I've ever seen!

 Recommended Hotel: **Casa de Lola Garcia**

JEFF & ALAN'S GUIDE TO MOTORCYCLE TRAVEL IN COLOMBIA

DAY 4 — Free Day in Salamina

Most travelers come to town and only get to see the beautiful architecture of the town. Lucky for us we have motorcycles and can travel into the backcountry outside Salamina and see some truly breathtaking landscapes. Today we take a trip over to the hamlet of San Felix and the nearby Samaria Valley. Here, growing on the slopes of lush green mountains, we find the national tree of Colombia, the Quindío Wax Palm. The wax palm is the tallest palm in the world, reaching heights of over four stories. Not only are the palms themselves beautiful, but they are home to green and yellow parrots, which can be seen flying overhead. The views across the valley are picture-perfect, and once you arrive, feel like you have somehow discovered a special place that hardly any other foreigner has set eyes upon.

> Recommended Hotel:
> **Casa de Lola Garcia**

The ride to the valley is as spectacular as the destination itself. The road out of Salamina takes us across a ridge with yet again, spectacular views of the town and the surrounding cloud forests with fog spilling over the treetops. The road is almost completely paved and makes for some easy riding before arriving in the small town of San Felix. San Felix is a pretty quiet place, and we won't see much activity other than the occasional local farmer wandering around the plaza dressed in his poncho and cowboy hat. This area is still relatively undiscovered, and it wouldn't be surprising if we were the only foreigners in town. Heading from San Felix to the wax palm forest, the road becomes unpaved but well maintained with hard-packed gravel. The ride to the palm forest is only 15 minutes and takes us through tropical forest and farmland with cows and horses dotting the lush green hillsides.

The wax palms of the Samaria Valley isn't the only sight to see. The surrounding area is filled with isolated off-road tracks that are perfect for riders wanting to explore more of the area. Visiting isolated towns such as Marulanda and Manzanares make great day trips if you wake up early. Continuing the drive south from Manzanares to the Nevado del Ruiz volcano is a great trip. Better yet, it keeps us out of the city traffic in Manizales. The ride is truly breathtaking and takes us through spectacular cloud forest landscapes with rolling fog spilling over the treetops.

 The Samaria Valley is the best alternative to the Cocora Valley in Colombia

DAY 5 — Salamina to Manizales

 Recommended Hotel:
Termales de Ruiz

NEVADO DEL RUIZ VOLCANO

Today takes us to the famous Nevado del Ruiz Volcano. Colombia is part of the Ring of Fire, a 40,000 kilometer (24,900 miles) long string of volcanoes that forms a horseshoe-shaped ring around the rim of the Pacific Ocean stretching into Asia. This Ring of Fire contains 75% of the world's volcanoes and 90% of its earthquakes with Colombia itself being home to 23 volcanoes, of which 19 are considered active. Conveniently located right in the heart of the coffee region is Nevado del Ruiz stratovolcano which reaches a staggering height of 5,311m (17,424ft).

Rides around the Nevado del Ruiz are often touted as "The best rides in Colombia." You'll ride up through the clouds until arriving in a high altitude tundra known as Páramo. Sitting at 13,000ft you will be surrounded by ancient plants that look a lot like cactus. Called frailejones these plants are actually related to sunflowers and are over 150 years old. Although you are at a high altitude the temperatures aren't freezing and the cool air feels more like a sunny day in the Swiss Alps than sitting on a stratovolcano on the equator.

Although beautiful, Nevado del Ruiz was the cause of one of the most devastating events in Colombian history. On November 13, 1985, after ignoring evacuation warnings from geologists, the Nevado del Ruiz erupted. The intense heat of the eruption melted the volcano's ice caps producing high-speed avalanches of mud, water, and debris (called lahars) that rushed down the side of the mountain destroying the town of Armero and claiming the lives of 23,080 of its residents.

This is Paramo, a high altitude tundra above the tree line

You can still visit the destroyed town of Armero and see abandoned buildings which are actually the upper levels of the town with the lower parts still covered with dirt.

HOTEL TERMALES DEL RUIZ

Whatever you do, don't even think of coming down from the volcano without spending at least one night at the Hotel Termales del Ruiz, one of the few hotels actually located on the side of an active volcano. Located amid stunning landscapes at 3500masl (11,500ft), this glorious thermal-bath complex is the place to go to for total relaxation. The ride to get here is just as good. Visiting this hotel means navigating an off-road route that takes you from the relatively low altitude of Manizales through the jungle and into the high altitude páramo. Built in the 1940s by a German skiing champion, the rooms have the feel of a classic alpine lodge because it actually was an alpine ski lodge, used by the first-ever Colombian ski-team. While not huge, the rooms are certainly comfortable.

Outside, there are two large hot thermal pools. Sitting in the steaming hot pools while feeling the cool mountain air and looking out over the valley below feels great after a long ride. The lodge is also great for bird watching. Located on a hillside above it, there's a birding shelter beside a gushing stream where 17 species of hummingbird come to feed including the second largest hummingbird species in the world. The front desk can provide you with brightly colored sugar water feeders to feed the birds from your hand.

Head uphill through a side road and you'll come to a forest of frailejones, a tundra plant that's been adapting at this altitude for eons, covering its flowers in white hairs to protect it from the sun and surrounding its stems in dead leaves to protect it from the cold.

Extend your trip: If you're interested in heading east to the Magdalena valley we recommend checking out the Alto de Los Letras. Alto de Los Letras is a giant among the mountain passes. Topping out at an elevation of 3.679m (12,070ft), the pass crosses the entire Central Cordillera of the Andes. Not only does it cross the entire mountain range but as you increase in altitude you are able to ride through basically all the climate zones in Colombia, from the hot tropical climate in Mariquita to an alpine glacier climate when you arrive at the Nevado del Ruiz Volcano.

DAY 6 — Manizales to Jardín

Jardín is the perfect place to finish a great trip. Leaving Nevado de Ruiz, we make our way down from the páramo and through the jungle until we reach the city of Manizales. Here we cross the city in about 30 minutes before we climb back up into the mountains towards the town of Riosucio. After reaching Riosucio the trail switches from pavement to unpaved gravel. We stay on the unpaved trail, winding our way through the forest until we reach the town of Jardín.

Revered for its brightly-colored houses and quaint mountainside location, Jardín is often dubbed 'the most beautiful town in all of Colombia' and acts as the poster-child for the culturally-enriched Antioquia region.

In Spring, when the town's floral decorations are in full bloom, Jardín is an explosion of colors (and tourists), and local cafes do a great job of reflecting the vibrant essence of the city with their rainbow-colored outdoor seating. The town looks tailor-made for postcards. In town, you can simply stroll the little colonial streets, admire the stunning architecture, and watch as cowboys come into town in the evening with their trained horses. The center of town is compact and easily explored on foot.

A great way to get a bird's eye view of the town is by cable-car. La Garrucha is a home built metal lattice cable car that pulls you across a valley while suspended hundreds of meters in the air. The views of the city, mountains, and valley below are incredible, and there is a restaurant located on the other side.

 Recommended Hotel:
Casa Passiflora Boutique Hotel

Visiting the Parque Natural Jardín de Rocas is a must-do trip for birdwatchers. You can see the shockingly bright orange and black Gallo de Roca Andino also known as the Andean Cock-Of-The-Rock. Located at what is known as a lek, we can see courtship displays with males trying to impress the females. The best time to go is in the early morning and just before dusk. You can get within feet of the birds as they socialize to start and end their days.

A hidden highlight of Jardín is found just outside the town, though: a magnificent spot called the Cave of Splendor (La Cueva del Esplendor). The best way to see this splendor is on a 12-mile hike, which is hard work but rewarding - you'll come face to face with a spectacular cave with a waterfall cascading right through its roof. You can enjoy a refreshing swim here, so pack your swimsuits. The cave is on private property, and there's a small charge to enter.

Jardin makes a great overnight trip from Medellín

JEFF & ALAN'S GUIDE TO MOTORCYCLE TRAVEL IN COLOMBIA

 Jardin is often dubbed 'the most beautiful town in all of Colombia

DAY 7 — Jardín to Medellín

🏢 Recommended Hotel: **Diez Hotel Categoria**

→ Jardin is the best place to see the brilliant red-orange Andean Cock-of-the-rock

Back to Medellín today! The trip from Jardín to Medellín takes around 4 hours and is all paved. A great place to stop and get lunch is the Santo Tomas Parrilla Bar. Located right on the road, the restaurant has fantastic views of the Cerro Tusa natural pyramid, Cerro Bravo, and the surrounding countryside. The people who serve are very friendly and the owner speaks English.

ColombiaMotoAdventures.com

Lost Emerald City

A unique experience to what was formerly the most dangerous place in Colombia. Deep in the rugged eastern portion of the Colombian Andes in the department of Boyaca lies the town of Muzo, known as the Emerald Capital of The World. Sealed off from the outside world for decades due to intense fighting, the area is now open after a peace treaty with the guerilla groups was signed.

Drive off-road through rugged terrain, cross mountain ranges, and streams, see amazing vistas and waterfalls, and finally get the chance to and interact with local emerald miners. You can even buy emeralds directly from the miners in the field!

Truly a once in a lifetime adventure and completely different than any other trip you have ever taken. The perfect group motorcycle adventure to hang out with your friends and experience a remote and rarely seen part of Colombia.

We've been there, it's safe and our clients find it one of the most interesting and fascinating places to discover. That being said, it's recommended that you speak fluent Spanish or go with a guide in order to find the mining area and communicate with the emerald miners.

Now grab some buddies and let's go explore Colombia on motorcycles!

HIGHLIGHTS

- Area now open for the first time in decades
- Mine for your own emeralds
- Buy emeralds from miners in the field
- Off-road motorcycle riding
- Remote towns and villages
- Majestic views around every corner

DAY 1 — Medellín to Landázuri

Leaving Medellín we wind our way through the mountains outside of the city. The road is paved the entire way and features gentle sweeping curves that are easy to handle. This is an easy way to begin the trip and get used to driving in Colombia. Once we drop into the tropical Magdalena valley the terrain becomes flat for the next few hours. Towering in the distance we begin to close in on a totally new mountain range, the rugged Eastern Andes. Here we begin to enter a tropical cloud forest where the temperature begins to cool off and is a welcome change compared to earlier in the day. Spending the night in the small town of Landázuri we can grab a bite to eat in the town square and prepare for the next day's ride.

For more than 4,000 years, emeralds have been among the most valuable of all jewels on Earth

Meeting emerald miners

An informal emerald miner, known as a guaquero, shows off some recently discovered emeralds.

DAY 2 — Landázuri to Windows of Tisquizoque

↑ It is estimated that Colombia accounts for 70-90% of the world's emerald market

Get ready for some rugged high-altitude riding. We are going to spend the entire day in the backcountry where the inhabitants rarely come into contact with foreigners. We'll repeatedly climb and descend through jagged mountains and valleys caused by a series of folded tectonic fault lines.

Guaranteed that you've never seen anything like this. Panoramic views are around every corner, and cold mist rolling through the landscape adds a "Lord of the Rings" dimension to the ride. Although the topography is rough, the roads are in surprisingly good shape consisting of well maintained hard-packed gravel.

We'll finish our journey on a road that snakes through a narrow canyon. Surrounded by steep rock walls on both sides we follow a winding river for miles before reaching our final destination, the town of Florián. The entire ride takes around five hours although stopping for photographs, coffee and food will turn it into an all-day ride.

DAY 3 — Windows of Tisquizoque to Muzo

Today we take the motorcycles to Muzo, the world capital of emeralds. Muzo is known not only for the number of emeralds it produces, but also for their superb quality and color with the Muzo mine producing the world's highest quality gems known for their warm, grassy-green color, with hints of yellow.

JEFF & ALAN'S GUIDE TO MOTORCYCLE TRAVEL IN COLOMBIA

DAY 4 Emerald Mining in Muzo

Today we visit the emerald miners. In the 1980s drug dealers fought the country's leading emerald mining families for rights to the emeralds. The mine owners fought back, turning Muzo into the most dangerous place in Colombia, and by the end of the decade, more than 6,000 people had been killed. Inevitably - as is often the case in Colombia - many of them were civilians caught up in the gun battles between rival paramilitary forces.

Now Muzo is a peaceful and beautiful place where we will be able to watch informal emerald miners known as guaqueros scour the river beds along the Itoco river in the Muzo valley in search of the precious stones. This is a great opportunity for documentary photography as well as a chance to speak with emerald miners about life in the mining camps and surrounding areas.

↑ Known as echando pala or "throwing the shovel" by the locals, miners scour the riverbed searching for emeralds

DAY 5 Muzo to Medellín

The adventure isn't over yet. Get ready for off-road motorcycle riding as we leave from Muzo and drive through the heart of the Colombian Emerald mining zone passing through the towns of Coscuez and Otanche. The area is extremely remote but at the same time very beautiful and awe-inspiring. We drop down from the mountain range and cross the plains of Colombia again before winding up into the mountain range of Medellín and ending the trip back home in the beautiful Aburrá valley.

↑ High pressure hoses are used to move the dark earth away and hopefully spot a gleaming emerald lying in the rough.

Journey To The Jungle

DAY 1 — Medellín to Sonsón

 Recommended Hotel: **El Tesoro**

This is going to be an interesting trip. Today we ride to the former guerilla conflict zone of Sonsón. Sonsón has been off-limits for decades due to guerilla activity. Although it's safe now there is very little information on the internet about the area. Consequently, it's untouched by tourism which makes it the perfect place to get an authentic taste of Colombia.

The ride to Sonsón is great. One of the best things about this ride is the miles and miles of exciting twists and turns. Ups, downs, ascending curves, descending curves, increasing radius curves, decreasing radius curves. You're going to get a ton of riding experience on just this one road. The pavement here is in good shape and as is the case in lots of areas in the countryside, there is very little traffic.

Midway we're going to stop off at Luisa's house and have a cup of local coffee called tinto. If you like kids you'll be delighted to meet her twin toddlers. Tourists never stop here and you'll see how happy she is to talk with us. Besides being a fun way to connect with the locals, it's a way to directly support a family business. We'll visit the HALO demining operations and learn about their efforts to remove leftover anti-personnel landmines from the area. We get the chance to hold deactivated landmines they have recovered. Yep, there are still landmines out here.

The town of Sonsón is located at a high elevation but we're going to climb even higher. The Páramo de Sonsón is a lookout point that stands at over 10,000ft in elevation. The lookout has a scenic view of the fog rolling across the cloud forest and nearby valley. By now it will be late afternoon and we'll head back to town to check in to our hotel and grab a pizza and a beer.

We stay at the El Tesoro hotel located on the main square. This is a 200-year-old mansion that has been converted into a unique hotel. Unlike other hotels, this one hasn't been updated and still retains its original charm. In addition, the hotel is somewhat of a museum and is filled with an eclectic collection of antiques. Looking over everything will keep you captivated for hours. Located next door to the hotel is a great pizza restaurant. From the second-story balcony, we can enjoy a brick oven pizza while people-watching on the main square. Sonsón leaves the warm weather of Guatapé behind. Located at 8,100ft you'll want to bring a jacket because it's going to be cold at night.

↑ A frog

HIGHLIGHTS

- **Beautiful** - Drive through the beautiful coffee country outside of Medellín and arrive in the town of Sonsón.
- **Coffee Market** - Drink coffee in the plaza while cowboys bring burros loaded with coffee to market
- **Remote Ecolodge** - Tube down the river, visit waterfalls while looking for wildlife.
- **River Crossing** - Put the bikes on a boat (or canoe) for a river crossing on the way back to Medellín!

DAY 2 — Sonsón to Norcasia

After breakfast, we ride to the Páramo de Sonsón lookout point that stands at over 10,000ft in elevation. The lookout has a beautiful view of the fog rolling across the forest and nearby valley and is a great way to start the day. We then take a winding road down into the rural coffee town of Narinó. We visit a local coffee cooperative where we see local farmers arriving with bags of coffee loaded on to mules. We learn how to sort, weigh and grade coffee and also have a chance to buy fresh coffee directly from the source. We can sit down in an authentic cafe to have a snack and drink tinto with the local coffee farmers and cowboys.

Recommended Hotel:
Termales Espiritu Santo

We then take a short off-road ride to the famous Espíritu Santo hot springs hotel. The trip takes us from the cool temperatures of the coffee region down into the dense jungle. Surrounded by thick jungle vegetation on both sides, the road is rough and unpaved, but that's what keeps the crowds away from this sweet spot. The hotel is a perfect place for having lunch, drinking a local fruit juice, and taking a dip in the hot springs or river before jumping back on the bikes and heading towards the town of Norcasia.

The road to Norcasia is also remote and unpaved, but the views make it worth the effort. Soon after leaving the hot springs, we cross a bridge over a river then start heading back into the mountains. On the way, we stop off at the remote village of Florencia. This village is so remote that there wasn't even a road leading to it until 1990. Once arriving here, you feel like you have entirely left the modern world behind. After passing through Florencia, we make the rest of the journey to Norcasia but not before making one final stop at the Mirador de Embalse Amaní, a spectacular lookout point above a huge jungle lake. Right after this, it's a quick ten-minute ride to Norcasia where we spend the night in town.

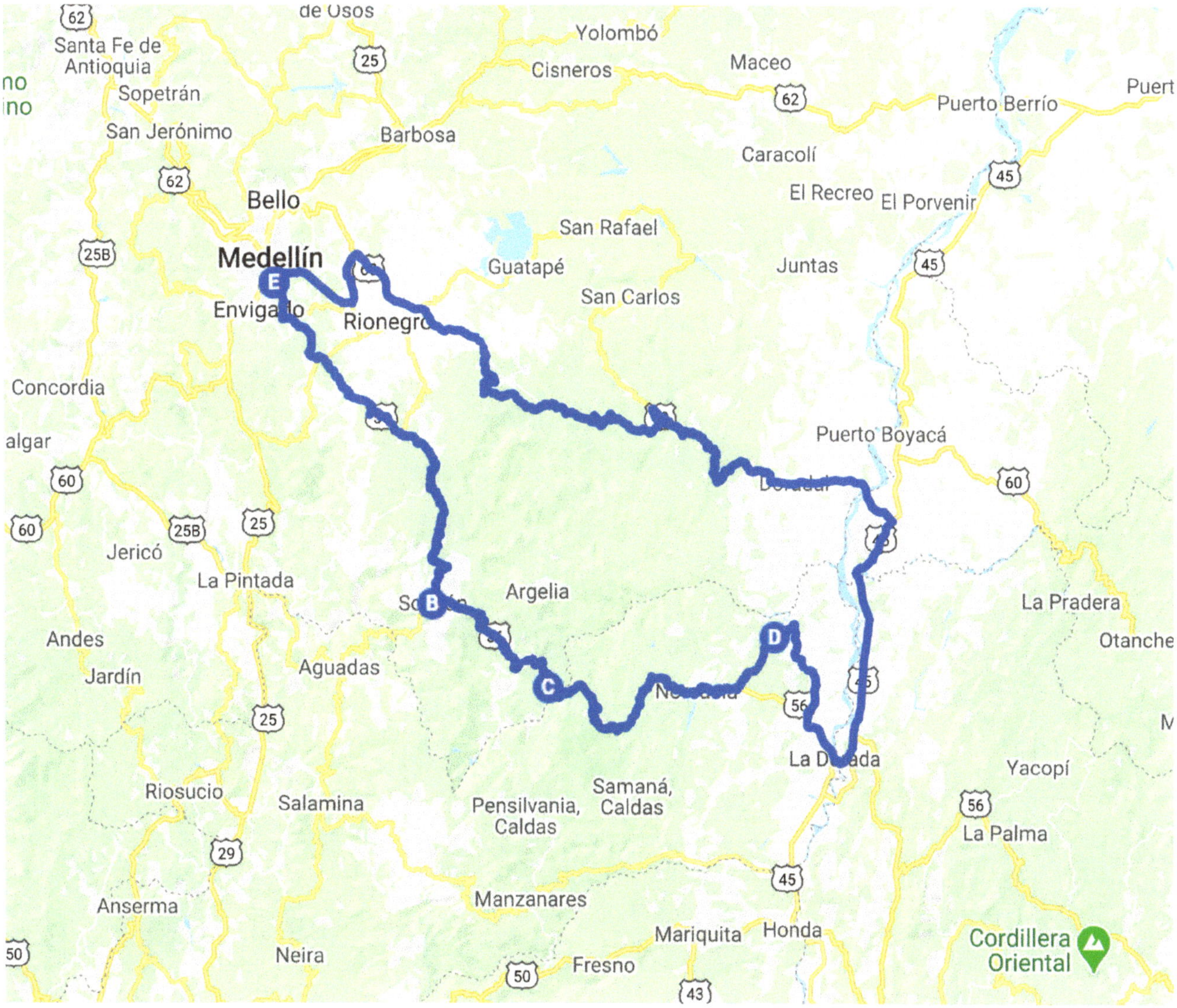

DAY 3 — Norcasia to La Chachaza

Set deep inside the jungle on the Miel River this lodge is amazing. A rough drive on a road made of dirt and loose rock takes us to a parking spot beside the Rio Miel. After arriving, a boat picks us up for a 5-minute ride up the Miel River to La Cachaza hotel. The hotel is surrounded by the jungle and has large tropical bamboo bungalows located on the river bank. The bungalows have open floor plans and are built with a local bamboo called guadua. The rooms have plenty of shade and very nice balconies and terraces with views of the river. All rooms come equipped with hammocks, nice beds with mosquito nets, large bathrooms and showers, and mini-refrigerators. The hotel also has wi-fi.

Depending on when we arrive, we can take a sunset boat trip down the river or spend the afternoon swimming in the crystal clear waters of the river. The food is simple fare from the region but very good. After dinner, we can drink cold beers, relax in the hammocks, or go for a walk to see the stars and the milky way. Sleeping here is a unique experience as we are surrounded by the fantastic sounds of the jungle at night.

Recommended Hotel:
Hotel Ecologico La Cachaza

It's easy to spot howler monkeys hanging out in trees by the river.

DAY 4 — Jungle Lodge - La Chachaza

Recommended Hotel:
Hotel Ecologico La Chachaza

Today we wake up and take a boat ride to some nearby waterfalls. The trip takes us through some beautiful scenery as well as a narrow rock canyon. On the way can spot water buffalo, otters, turtles, howler monkeys as well as many types of birds such as cranes, toucans, and osprey among many others. Spend a relaxing time bathing in the waterfall and swimming in the plunge pool. Afterward, we take innertubes and float down the river on the way back to the ecolodge. In the evening we have a chance to take another sunset boat ride and relax on the boat as we look for wildlife and swim in the river.

On our way to visit spectacular waterfalls and tube down the river.

DAY 5 — San Miguel River Crossing to Guatapé

Today we make our way to the town of Guatapé but first, we need to cross a river. After a short off-road ride, we arrive at the town of San Miguel. Here we load the bikes onto a car barge or, depending on the water level, canoes. We then made the short trip across the river and continued on our way to Guatapé. The river crossing is a nice experience and is an important shortcut and saves us hours of driving. We spend the rest of the morning riding off-road through the cattle country of the Magdalena valley before jumping back on pavement for the ride towards Cocorná.

On the way to Guatapé, we make a stop for lunch at the Katarata restaurant near the town of Cocorná. The restaurant offers amazing views of the valley and great food. You can also watch paragliders fly by your table as well as circle around a nearby waterfall. The paragliding company is conveniently located next door to the restaurant. If you decide to fly we recommend eating lunch after the flight.

After lunch, we wind down into the valley where we take narrow backroad trails through the countryside on the way to Guatapé.

The big draw here is the famous Piedra del Peñol and the view of the lake and surrounding area from the top. The Piedra is a high granite monolith (technically an inselberg) that rises from near the edge of a man-made lake called the Embalse Guatapé. A brick staircase of 659 steps rises up through a broad fissure on the side of the rock. From the top, you'll soak up magnificent views of this fertile region, the fingers of the lake sprawling amid a vast expanse of green mountains.

JEFF & ALAN'S GUIDE TO MOTORCYCLE TRAVEL IN COLOMBIA

DAY 6 — Guatapé - Medellín

Recommended Hotel:
Hotel Ecologico La Chachaza

You'll probably want to wake up early today, so you can climb up the stairs of stunning Piedra del Penol and soak up morning views from the top. Lovely Guatapé is one of the most popular day-trip options from Medellín and it's a place that never fails to impress. At the top of the monolith, you'll find a three-story viewing platform and souvenir shop - the peak can get crowded during the day so arriving first thing means you avoid the big crowds, especially if visiting on the weekend.

The ride to Medellín takes around two hours on a paved road and is fairly uneventful if there isn't any traffic. Starting about an hour after leaving Guatapé you will notice that the traffic begins to get heavier. Highway congestion from busses and people returning to Medellín can make the highway more challenging. The last leg of the trip dropping into Medellín's valley is a bit steeper so be sure to watch your speed and increase your following distance.

ColombiaMotoAdventures.com 119

More Than A Week

JEFF & ALAN'S GUIDE TO MOTORCYCLE TRAVEL IN COLOMBIA

Journey to the Center of the Earth - Medellín to Quito, Ecuador

This trip takes the popular coffee region loop and extends it all the way to the Ecuadorian capital of Quito, before returning north through a different route. With very little backtracking, a sensational array of unique experiences, and plenty of time to dig a little deeper into the history, culture, and wilderness of this astonishing region of South America, this 19-day trip to "The Center of the Earth" is that perfect trip you've been searching for.

ColombiaMotoAdventures.com

HIGHLIGHTS

- **Two Countries, One Trip** - Ride a motorcycle from Medellín, Colombia then cross the border into Ecuador on a trip to stand on the equator.

- **Climb The Rock** - Soak up "the most spectacular views in Colombia" from the top of famous Piedra del Peñol in Guatapé, with its 740-step stairway to the heavens

- **Páramo** - Fantastic high-altitude riding across the Colombian tundra called Páramo, one of the world's rarest and most bio-diverse ecosystems – enjoy the country's longest road ascent!

- **Devils Trampoline** - Often touted as one of the world's most dangerous roads, this is a biker's ultimate bucket-list adventure!

- **Hot Springs** - Soak up your weary bones in the sublime therapeutic hot springs flanking the glaciated Nevado del Ruiz Volcano, at an altitude of 3,500masl

- **Visit The Equator** - Stand on the spot located right outside of Ecuador's capital.

- **Wax Palm Forest** - Take a stroll through the otherworldly Wax Palm Forest of the Cocora Valley, home to the tallest palm trees on earth

- **Scenery** - Enjoy the kind of sensory overload that can only be experienced when riding through a kaleidoscope of landscapes, altitudes, and climates

DAY 1 — Medellín - Aerial Tram and Parque Lleras

Medellín is undoubtedly the one Colombian city that's undergone the most drastic change in the last two decades and now shines resplendent as a beacon of tourism in the country. Like a bad kid turned really, really good, the city entices over 2.5 million tourists a year nowadays, with its young, dynamic, laid-back, and arty vibe. The Wall St Journal named Medellín the "Most Innovative City in the World" way back in 2013.

This is a great city to explore for a few days before the start of your tour!

Medellín is one of the most picturesque cities in Latin America, set in a deeply carved valley and surrounded by verdant peaks – the view, from afar, is out of this world. We recommend spending the day flying over the city on the aerial tram on the way to have lunch in Parque Arvi. At night we recommend drinking some rum and people watching in Parque Lleras

DAY 2 — Medellín to Jardín
(130km / 80mi)

Jardín, which is Spanish for 'garden', feels like it was plucked right out of a Western film set, complete with poncho and sombrero-wearing llaneros and a ridiculously charming main plaza framed by rustic bars and local eateries. From the moment you get off your bike, you'll realize that everything about Jardín is authentic. Take a leisurely stroll around the main plaza of El Libertador Park, take a moment to smell the bright pink roses in the manicured garden, and ascend the bell-tower of the neo-Gothic Basilica of the Immaculate Conception, for breath-taking views. Have we mentioned the local melt-in-your-mouth milk candies yet?

JEFF & ALAN'S GUIDE TO MOTORCYCLE TRAVEL IN COLOMBIA

DAY 3 — Jardín to Manizales
(128km / 79mi) - Hot Springs and Páramo

Recommended Hotel:
Termales de Ruiz

This longer itinerary south brings you to those sensational thermal baths high up on the side of Nevado del Ruiz Volcano. Enjoy the coolness of the higher altitude because you'll be heating up in no time after this!

DAY 4 — Manizales to Cali
(260km / 161mi)

Recommended Hotel:
Hotel Ecologico La Chachaza

Today, kick it up a notch and head off early for the first of your long ride days. The road to Cali, from Manizales, is dotted with fantastic reasons to stop – all conveniently placed about an hour's ride away. Stop by the northern shores of Lago Calima Valle for a refreshing swim. Bypass bustling Tulua and, instead, stop in the quaint town of Buga, one of Colombia's oldest towns and a crazy-popular religious pilgrimage site.

Cali is renowned as Colombia's salsa capital (that'll be the dance, not the dip!) and the hypnotic beat of Latin America's favorite music permeates every corner of the city. Lively bars, street dancing, a modest Christ statue sitting atop a hill boasting great views, a quirky park filled with over-sized cat-statues, world-class food, jaw-dropping churches, and outstanding wilderness just outside the city are a few of the highlights awaiting your arrival.

DAY 5: Cali to Popayan
(141km / 87mi)

A shorter yet more dramatic ride-day awaits you today, as you start your climb up the Andes to reach the lesser-visited town of Popayán.

Dubbed The White City of Colombia, Popayan is a maze of white-washed houses an unmistakable hint that this was, in the early 19th century, one of the most prominent trading posts between Colombia and Ecuador.

Impeccably preserved and rated second-best in Colombia only after Cartagena, Popayán is the first destination we hit that's way off the usual touristy path. Easy to navigate on foot and more-than-a-little blinding on a sunny day, the historic center is an architecture buff's Utopia and boasts the highest concentration of churches in all of Colombia. Recognized by UNESCO as a gastronomic hub bar none, Popayan is known for its potato empanadas (empanadas de pipián), usually served with a spicy peanut sauce.

DAY 6 — Popayán to Pasto
(257km / 160)

The Popayán to Pasto road is undoubtedly one of the most magnificent in all of Colombia so make sure the sky is crystal clear before setting off. Given that both cities boast impressive altitudes, on opposite sides of the mountains, you can expect a truly epic ride day through what is, essentially, one of the most overlooked and underrated regions of Colombia.

Pasto is a pleasant mountain town that's set in the high-altitude Atriz Valley and boasts an interesting history. The most enticing aspect, however, is the amazing Andean nature that surrounds it.

Nearby is Cumbal, the southernmost active volcano in Colombia (which stands at a breath-taking 4764masl – 15,630ft) and the main reason discerning mountaineers head here in droves.

DAY 7 — Pasto to Ipiales (118km / 73mi) - Las Lajas Sanctuary

The road to Ipiales (2,950masl – 9,678ft) is a biker's dream: we're talking over 100km of non-stop mountain curves, just the thing to get our adrenalin pumping.

Ipiales sits just north of the border with Ecuador and is particularly famous thanks to the nearby Sanctuary of the Virgin of Las Lajas, perhaps Colombia's most Insta-famous churches. The spectacular cathedral, intricately carved and with a richly decorated décor, was built on the side of a steep and narrow gorge above the Guaitará River, and is shrouded in mystical local lore.

Whether you're a believer (or not) matters little: the architecture and preposterous location of the church and its picturesque bridge make it an unmissable sight.

↑ Las Lajas is a gorgeous church, built on a bridge in the middle of a canyon

DAY 8 — Ipiales to Chachimbiro
(141km / 87Mi)
Border cross into Ecuador

Border crossing day! Your ride is not too long today although it's always best to tackle the usual border-crossing rigmarole early in the morning. Once in Ecuador (high-fives all-round), you can head straight for the thermal spring resort town of Chachimbiro, one of the least known and most enjoyable of all the thermal towns in this northern region of Ecuador.

Locals are huge believers of the healing power of natural thermal pools and really, after a week of riding the Andes of southern Colombia. So spend the afternoon soaking your weary bones and the scenery, and feasting on fried tilapia.

 The "Middle of the Earth" exhibit in Quito, Ecuador

DAY 9 — Chachimbiro to Quito
(135km / 84mi) Equator crossing day!

Zoom in and explore Quito with this gigapixel panorama. https://www.gigapixelquito.com

The Ecuadorian capital is, in many respects, one of Latin America's most appealing cities. Its setting is drop-dead gorgeous and its historic core as close to postcard-perfect as you could get. Yet it's the distinct lack of tourist crowds, outside the main commercial drag of New Town, that makes it so enjoyable.

On your way to Quito, this morning, stop by Ciudad Mitad del Mundo, the somewhat cheesy but certainly entertaining City in the Middle of the World that denotes the crossing of the Equator. Quito sits at an altitude of 2,850masl (9,350ft) and is overshadowed by Cotopaxi Volcano, the second-highest peak in Ecuador (5,897masl – 19,247ft) and one of the most active in all of South America. Once you're all settled in and refreshed, take the teleférico (cable car) to Pichincha for a bird's eye view that'll blow you away; get lost in the cobbled maze of Old Town Centre and spend your evening strolling along Calle La Ronda and its wonderful array of food, souvenir and craft stalls.

DAY 10 — Quito to Otavalo (92KM / 57Mi)
Otavalo Market

↑ Colorful blankets at the Otavalo market

Today, make a U-turn back up towards Colombia, not before stopping by the northern town of Otavalo, revered for its Saturday artisan market that attracts indigenous sellers and buyers from all over northern Ecuador. Brightly colored pottery and hand-woven fabrics are the best buys to nab here (and reason to leave half your bike-bags empty!) but the most memorable experience will surely come from your dealings with local sellers.

A visit to Otavalo offers a glimpse into the more traditional and rural side of Ecuadorian life. Located 50 miles north of Quito, the valley is populated by some 45,000 Indians. Women with their distinctive long plaits and men with their colorful ponchos and fedoras, are among the most photogenic in South America. The Otavaleño's weaving skills are legendary and the amazing popularity of their wares, with foreign visitors, has helped them keep their cultural traditions alive.

DAY 11 — Otavalo to Ipiales (167km / 104mi)
Border cross into Colombiay

↑ Nevado Cotopaxi - Yes there is snow on the equator

We return to Ipiales today on what is, essentially, the only back-tracking you'll do on this entire motorcycle journe

DAY 12 — Ipiales to Mocoa – Devil's Trampoline (218km / 135mi)

The Devil's Trampoline is often touted as one of the world's most dangerous roads: a 70km (43mi)-long stretch of winding, unpaved and narrow track that seems to float in a consistent layer of eerie fog. Riding a motorcycle along this stretch of road towards Mocoa is possibly the main reason to choose this itinerary and, let us assure you, this hair-raising road with its blind corners and 1000 ft. drop-offs, will not disappoint. This is a biker's ultimate bucket-list adventure!

The road isn't as utterly insane as it was just a few years back. Today, a few well-placed guardrails and colossal DANGER! signs do make you feel just a tad more secure.

The Devils Trampoline is filled with blind corners is made more dangerous by fog and periodic washouts

By mid-afternoon, you should be sweating buckets in Mocoa, one of the many gateways to Colombia's luscious Amazon rainforest. With a smattering of wonderful waterfalls, jungle hikes, and eco-adventure sports, there'll be plenty to keep you busy here for the rest of the day.

DAY 13 — Mocoa to San Augustin (145km / 90mi)

One day at low-altitude was enough, right? We hope so! After a hearty breakfast of fried eggs and plantain chips, saddle up and head back up those addictive Andes again, aiming for one of Colombia's most fascinating, UNESCO-listed archaeological sites. San Agustin Archaeological Park is bursting with pre-Colombian statues – huge carved stone statues that look like they are from Easter Island in the Pacific. This place is straight out of an Indiana Jones movie my friends! First up, spend a bit of time in the little museum found at the entrance of the park, and then take one of the many walking trails that guides you to the main part of the park, where clusters of statues and monuments are all within easy walking distance.

The remnants of a mysterious ancient culture that flourished between the 1st and the 8th century BC

DAY 14 — San Augustin to Tatacoa Desert (269km / 167mi)

The Tatacoa Desert is Colombia's second-largest dry area in Colombia after the desert of La Guajira and boasts one of Colombia's most ethereal landscapes. Due to the lack of light pollution and clear, dry air, Tatacoa is renowned for offering world-class stargazing and home to one of the country's premier observatories.

Reminiscent of the Badlands of South Dakota, the landscape is a maze of heavily eroded dry canyons and gullies. Exploring the dry desert place on motorcycles is a once-in-a-lifetime experience as is the chance to spend an evening stargazing in the company of avid astronomers. The Tatacoa observatory is open to the public although, if you simply wish to swing in a hammock and watch the sparkling lights, you can do that too.

DAY 15 — Tatacoa Desert to Mariquita (350km / 217 mi)

Leaving the desert landscapes behind we head to the town of Mariquita. The town makes the perfect stopping point before tackling the high altitude ride to Salamina the next day. The road to Mariquita is fairly uneventful and is basically a straight shot on the highway, but there are some interesting stops along the way.

The temperatures will remain high as we transit the Magdalena valley. The trip will be a 5 hour all paved ride. During the final stretch of the trip, we stop at the site of Colombia's most tragic natural disaster, the Armero Tragedy. In 1985 the dormant Nevado del Ruiz Volcano erupted near the town of Armero. Recommendations to evacuate the community were ignored by politicians and town residents were not even warned about the eruption. The eruption caused a pyroclastic mudslide that destroyed the town of Armero and killed over 20,000 people who were sleeping in their beds. Today, Armero is a ghost town with the lower stories of buildings buried beneath the ground and only upper levels are visible.

On the final approach to our destination lies the crystal clear Medina Falls. A perfect place to go for a swim and cool off if you're so inclined. There are several nice hotels in town that have swimming pools so if you're not up to drive to the waterfalls you can simply relax at the hotel pool.

JEFF & ALAN'S GUIDE TO MOTORCYCLE TRAVEL IN COLOMBIA

DAY 16
Mariquita to Salamina
(188km / 117mi)

There are two routes to get to Salamina from Mariquita. The first one is the Alto de Letras, which is known as the longest road climb in the Americas due to its length and altitude. Topping out at an altitude of 3.692m (12,112ft), the paved road takes you from the tropics to an alpine climate in just a few hours. Not only does it cross the entire mountain range but as you increase in altitude you are able to ride through basically all the climate zones in Colombia, from the hot tropical climate in Mariquita to an alpine glacier climate when you arrive at the Nevado del Ruiz Volcano. It's a beautiful ride but can be a little complicated due to truck traffic and tight corners. The weather can be cold, rainy, and foggy so bringing rain gear is absolutely mandatory. Don't even think of going up there without it. After coming down from the pass you can stop for the night at a hot springs hotel in Manizales or spend time navigating through the city before taking the three hour drive north to Salamina.

The second route, my personal favorite, is like riding through motorcycle heaven. Taking back roads from Mariquita to Salamina you begin a

 **Recommended Hotel:
Casa de Lola Garcia**

spectacular journey winding your way through central Andes. The road consists of hundreds of twists and turns crossing countless mountain passes and valleys. The trip lasts 6 hours and takes you through some of the most beautiful landscapes in Colombia. The road starts out as paved but changes to an unpaved packed gravel road after the town of Manzanares taking you through cool climates and lush vegetation.

Salamina is Colombia's best-kept secret. Tucked away in a far off corner of the coffee region, the beauty of Salamina is a sight to behold. The town itself is situated on the peak of a mountain, with entire streets sometimes appearing as if they are about to slide off the side of the mountain. Once we enter the town, we see why it has earned national heritage status. Houses climb the sloping streets with each one determined to outdo its neighbors. Elaborate woodworking takes the form of intricately decorated doors, windows, balconies, and zócalos (the distinct lower sections of the whitewashed facades). It's hard to walk the streets of Salamina without constantly looking upward at the flower-filled balconies.

A gorgeous bronze basin fountain made in Paris sits in the central plaza surrounded by tall trees and benches. In 1900 the fountain was brought to town on the backs of oxen and mules and since then it has become a symbol of the region. There are also various restaurants surrounding the main square where you can try typical local dishes, including the local favorite of steamed eggs (Huevos al Vapor), which is made with the help of an espresso machine.

One of the nicer boutique options in Salamina is the Casa de Lola Garcia. Formerly a coffee hacienda, the owners have beautifully restored the house and converted it into a charming boutique hotel. The property is complete with spacious rooms, king-sized beds, and a beautiful courtyard with jasmine trees and a jacuzzi. The hotel has a perfect location and is only a two-minute walk from the main square.

DAY 17 — Salamina to Sonsón
(87km / 54mi)

Today we ride to the former guerilla conflict zone of Sonsón. Sonsón has been off-limits for decades due to guerilla activity. Although it's safe now there is very little information on the internet about the area. Consequently, it's untouched by tourism which makes it the perfect place to get an authentic taste of Colombia. We'll even meet some people conducting demining operations and learn about their efforts to remove leftover anti-personnel landmines from the area. You'll get the chance to hold deactivated landmines that have been recovered. Yep, there are still landmines out here. This is a rare opportunity that you won't get in any other country in the region.

This ride is rugged and will be all off-road, but not difficult or technical. Some sections may be a little steep

Recommended Hotel:
El Tesoro

and other sections may have gravel. There will be some significant altitude changes and the going will be slower due to changing unpaved road surfaces. The route takes us through bamboo forest, banana plantations, and once we get higher, through coffee farms.

The town of Sonsón is located at a high elevation but we're going to climb even higher. The Páramo de Sonsón is a lookout point that stands at over 10,000ft in elevation. The lookout has a scenic view of the fog rolling across the cloud forest and nearby valley. By now it will be late afternoon and we'll head back to town to check in to our hotel and grab a pizza and a beer.

We stay at the El Tesoro hotel located on the main square. This is a 200-year-old mansion that has been converted into a unique hotel. Unlike other hotels, this one hasn't been updated and still retains its original charm. In addition, the hotel is somewhat of a museum and is filled with an eclectic collection of antiques. Looking over everything will keep you captivated for hours.

Located next door to the hotel is a great pizza restaurant. From the second-story balcony, we can enjoy a brick oven pizza while people-watching on the main square. Sonsón leaves the warm weather of Guatapé behind. Located at 8,100ft you'll want to bring a jacket because it's going to be cold at night.

JEFF & ALAN'S GUIDE TO MOTORCYCLE TRAVEL IN COLOMBIA

DAY 18

Sonsón to Guatapé
(140km / 87mi) -
Climb the Rock

 Recommended Hotel: **Zocalo Campestre**

The gorgeous town of Guatapé is a leisurely 2hr-ride away from Medellín (paved all the way) and makes for a fantastic 'lunch' outing and makes for a great intro to touring Colombia.

It's safe to say that pretty much all the towns in Colombia are beautiful and this one is no exception; the only difference is that here you can visit the famous Piedra del Peñol. This high granite monolith (technically an inselberg) rises from near the edge of a man-made lake, the Embalse Guatapé. A brick staircase of 659 steps rises up through a broad fissure on the side of the rock. From the top, you'll soak up magnificent views of this fertile region, the fingers of the lake sprawling amid a vast expanse of green mountains.

After coming down, find a spot in the restaurant below, that boasts a view of the lake. Order up a huge bandeja paisa complete with beans, rice, chorizo and avocado, and of course a cold beer or guanabana juice.

Some tourist attractions are just too good to ignore!

DAY 19

Guatapé to Medellín
(100km /62mi)

The day no-one ever looks forward to! This morning, after a lazy breakfast, you can head home to Medellín and bring this unforgettable adventure to an end. As you may already know, the best way to tackle the post-trip blues is to get stuck into the planning of the next one!

Medellín-Cartagena Loop

Cartagena is right at the top of many rider's must-visit lists and we've got four itinerary suggestions, each one offering different highlights and varying degrees of riding difficulty. The straightest distance is about 640km (400mi) and although it's possible to do it in a day - you'll definitely want to avoid that if you have the time to slow it down and enjoy the journey.

WEST - MUTATA (NATIONAL ROUTE 62) – This is the straightest route west to the coast and is ideal if you'd love to reach the beaches in the shortest time possible and then meander up the coast, visiting all those charming seaside villages up to Cartagena. This is also the route you'd take to Panama, via Turbo, but you don't need to opt for this only if planning a crossing of the Darién Gap – the islands of Capurganá and surrounds are fab to visit of their own accord.

NORTH - CAUCASIA (NATIONAL ROUTE 25) - AKA the boring option that Google maps suggests. Fast and efficient if you're short on time but, although the initial stretch out of Medellín takes you into high-altitude areas with mountain passes at 8500ft, it then drops down towards the coast, and this long stretch of straight can get a little boring.

EAST - RUTA DEL SOL (HIGHWAY 45) - Ruta del Sol is a motorway route that will take you almost to Santa Marta - a good option if you want to reach the far north-west and then slowly meander down the coast, to and past Cartagena, then Turbo and, finally, pick up the 62 back to Medellín. Great option if you'd like to do a loop trip.

If you have a lot of time, you can head south into Ecuador, back up, then east into the Andes and north-west to the coast. Yes, we realize this pretty much covers all of Colombia and would take a month, at least, and that would be the priceless point!

CARTAGENA?

The pearl of the Caribbean and Colombia's most celebrated colonial-era town, Cartagena is as beautiful as you've always been led to believe. We don't even care how busy it gets – there's never a wrong time of year to spend a couple of days meandering the historic center, meeting its colorful locals, and feasting on its delicious pargo frito, a dish of fried fish served with coconut rice is reason alone to visit. Known as Colombia's party central, Cartagena is all about languid days spent lying on postcard-worthy beaches, and nights spent dancing and drinking with new local friends.

↑ Necocli is the perfect jumping off point for trips to Caribbean coast

DAY 1

Medellín to Necoclí -
45km / 30mi

↑ The photogenic Puente de Occidente bridge in Santa Fe de Antioquia.

The trip to Necoclí takes a full day and is a natural stopping point for anyone wanting to visit the small towns on the coast before driving north to Cartagena. The ride to Necoclí is fairly uneventful. The trip takes you from the mountains of Medellín and drops you into the hot flat farmlands of Colombia. After endless hours of driving through banana plantations, you will finally arrive in Necoclí. If you wake up early the ride can be done in one day but if you want to break up the trip we recommend stopping in the small town of Mutata. The trip isn't scenic or eventful but if you want to get to the beautiful coast it's necessary to cross this area. The town of Necoclí itself isn't that spectacular either but it makes the perfect place to park your bike for a day or two and take a boat to the remote beach town of Capurganá.

JEFF & ALAN'S GUIDE TO MOTORCYCLE TRAVEL IN COLOMBIA

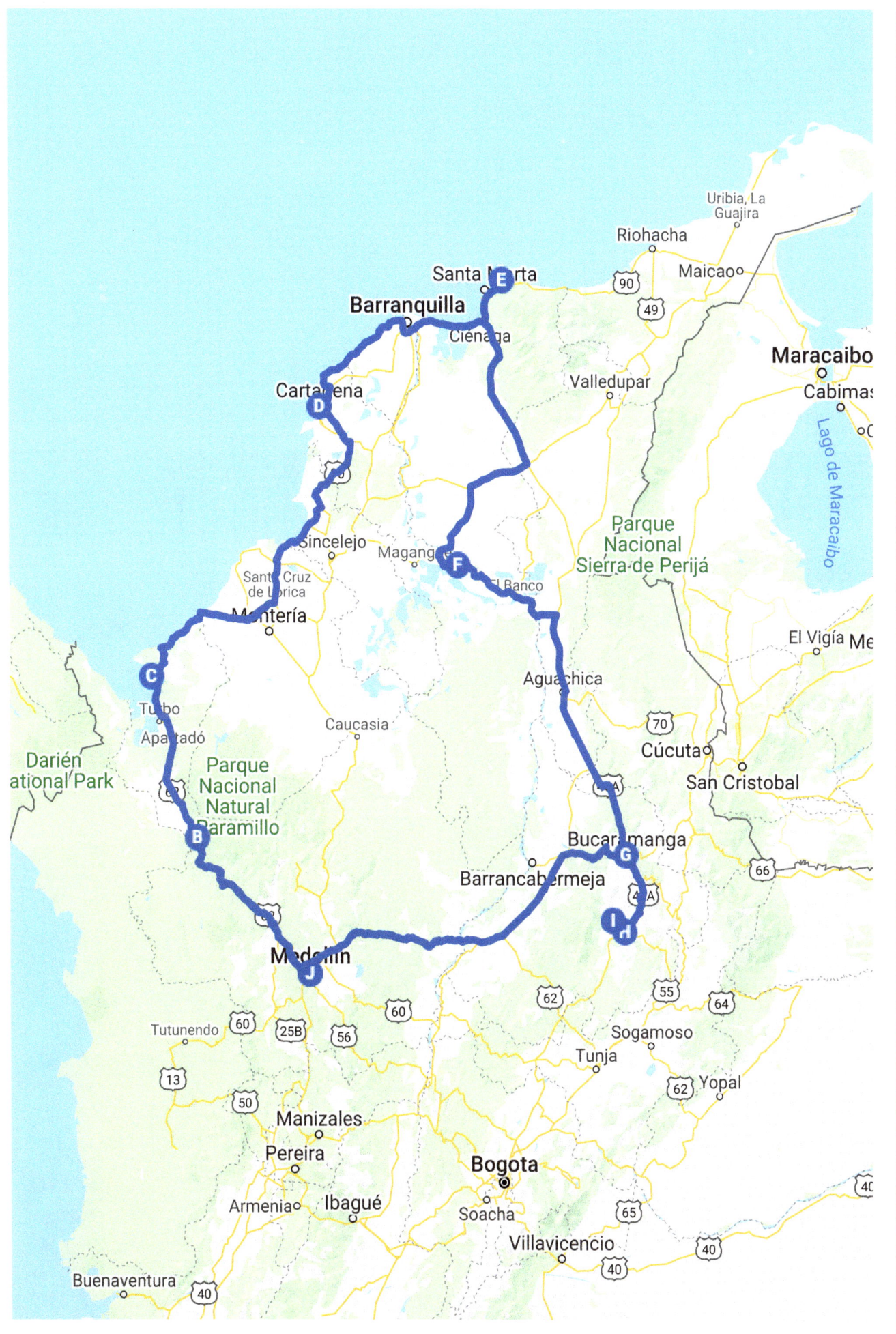

DAY 2

Necoclí to Capurganá

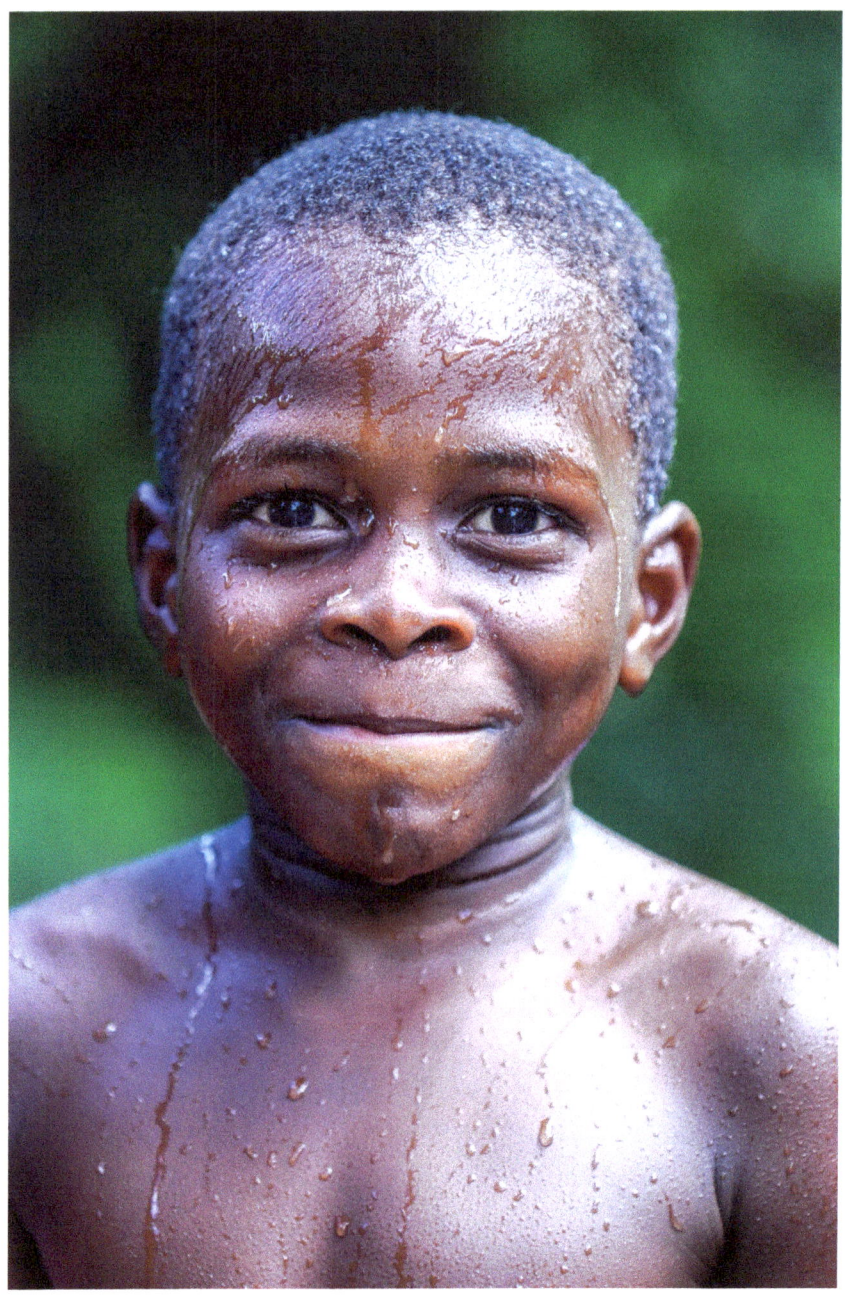

I f you're looking for a coastal beach town, flip flops in the sand, and rum in the tiki hut type of place, Capurganá is more authentic and laid back than Santa Marta or Cartagena with their endless t-shirt shops and street hustlers. Accessible only by sea or plane, what Necoclí lacks in seaside charm, Capurganá more than makes up for! Known for quiet bays backed by dense rainforest and abundant dive sites, Capurganá is the perfect place to spend a few days off the grid. Speaking of being off the grid, be sure to bring enough money for your stay as there is no ATM machine in the area.

One of the most popular activities is walking into Panama and visiting the town of La Miel. The trip offers fantastic views of the two villages as well as the emerald green rainforest and sapphire ocean. The hike passes through the town of Sapzurro and takes around two hours. The trip isn't too difficult although if it recently rained we recommend wearing boots for the mud. Once you arrive you will find seafood restaurants, crystal clear water, and white sand beaches.

DAY 3 (OR 4 OR 5)

Necoclí to Cartagena- 378km/235mi

Once you've hit the coast and are heading up to Cartagena, the options are literally endless. If you took a few days out in Capurganá, and are running out of time, you can knock out this stretch in one very long day.

SANTA CRUZ DEL ISLOTE - Want to have a totally cool story to bring back home? Head over to the island of Santa Cruz del Islote. This remote place holds the title of being the most densely populated island on the planet with a population of 1200 people living on an island the size of two football fields. If you have a drone this island makes for an amazing photo to hang on your wall. To get here you can take a boat from the towns of Rincón del Mar, Tolú or from Cartagena.

EXPLORE THE ISLANDS - Rincón del Mar is the perfect place to relax for a few days or to catch a speedboat to the San Bernardo Islands. Múrcura, in particular, hosts stunning bioluminescent plankton as well as small hotels that are basically tiny rock islands in the middle of the ocean. Isla Palma is another island in the area and is known for lots of fish and great snorkeling.

COVEÑAS - For a more up-scale trip, hit Coveñas instead, the most popular beach resort town in the Gulf of Morrosquillo. Coveñas has all you need for a few days of relaxing beach-bumming: long stretches of beach, water sport options, shallow surf, and great ceviche. Don't forget to leave time for a longboat tour of the Caimanera wetlands next door, a prized mangrove system home to many caimans, tropical birds, and other exotic wildlife.

DAY 5 & 6 Cartagena

Don't Party Like The Secret Service - Colombia is known as the "Thailand of Latin America for its availability of prostitutes and if partying had a capital city, Cartagena would be it. Just ask the US Secret Service! Back in 2012, about 17 secret service agents and 5 members of the US special forces were sent to Cartagena as part of President Obama's advanced security detail. After checking in at the famous Hotel Caribe, they spent the week drinking, going to clubs where they picked up around 20 prostitutes. Everything would have gone ok except one of the Secret Service agents got into an argument with a prostitute over his "bill for services." The girl said that she was owed $800USD but the agent said that it was only $47USD. The argument got really heated causing the police to be called and resulting in the biggest public relations disaster in the security team's history. We definitely recommend staying away from a place called Pleyclub due to the large amounts of prostitutes, and alcohol found there.

↑ Parque Tayrona is stunningly beautiful but is limited to a certain number of visitors per day You can buy a ticket at the main entrance of the park.

ROOFTOP POOLS - While you're not busy avoiding partying and prostitutes at night are lots of things to do during the day such as going to luxury hotels and purchasing day passes to hangout at their rooftop bars and pools.

BIOLUMINESCENT PLANKTON TOUR - When in Cartagena, you'll have the chance to check out one of nature's most intriguing phenomena. Take a boat tour to Puerto Naito Baru to swim among bioluminescent plankton. Pick a moonless, starry evening and enjoy an amazing experience, swimming in complete darkness with only the glow of the blue light emitted being from the plankton.

TOTUMO MUD VOLCANO - Another cool thing to do is going for a swim in the naturally heated Totumo mud volcano which is about 45 minutes outside of Cartagena.

DAY 7 — Cartagena to Santa Marta & Tayrona National Park
- 146KM/ 91MI

From here, you can hook up your itinerary with a visit to spectacular Tayrona. If you're after a truly spectacular place to take a dip in the Caribbean, then you can (almost) skip the whole above-mentioned lot and head straight up to Tayrona from Medellín instead. This protected reserve encompasses the wildest and least developed stretch of Colombia's northern coast – an incredible coastal jungle that literally crashes into the sea in spectacular form – we're talking dreamy beaches framed by rows of palm trees, quiet coves, unspoiled beaches, and the kind of coastal landscape that's made every guide-book cover the world over.

TREK LA CIUDAD PERDIDA – THE LOST CITY TREK

Ready to play Indiana Jones? Believed to be almost 700 years older than Machu Picchu, the real Lost City of the Andes is one of Colombia's most spectacular rising stars and we bet the trek to get there will soon-enough outrank even the famed Inca Trail in Peru. Nestled in the northern wilds of the Santa Marta Mountains, the Lost City is an amazing trip. A multi-day trek means putting up with heat, bugs, and rain - yet the rewards are out of this world. Among an ecosystem that's pristine and unspoiled, you'll be ankle-deep in rivers and taking refreshing plunges in waterfalls not many even know exist, you'll learn all about the tropical flora and will meet indigenous tribes still living here, unperturbed by the encroaching modernity, and always willing to lend a hand and a smile. This is not an easy challenge, but nothing that's unforgettable ever is.

OPTIONAL ROUTE -

TAYRONA TO CABO DE LA VELA - 428km / 266mi

If you have the luxury of more time and don't need to loop back to Medellín just yet, continue north to the cape and the northeasternmost point in all of Colombia. A windsurfing and kitesurfing mecca, this windy but jaw-dropping region of Colombia is remote and hard to reach but absolutely spellbinding. We're talking extremely hot and dry desert trails, overlooking sapphire seas, and very few towns to get in your way.

DAY 8 — Cartagena to Santa Cruz to Mompox - 328KM / 200MI

Mompox is known as the anti-Cartagena due to the fact that very few travelers visit the area. Mompox is a place of unparalleled architectural beauty and seemingly frozen in time. Founded in 1540, the town was once a center of wealth and trade and rivaled Cartagena in importance as a port. Once the giant Magdelena river changed its course and riverboats were diverted elsewhere, the town lost its importance as a trade hub. Named a UNESCO world heritage site in 1995, Mompox is said to be the closest you can get to experiencing life in a colonial-era port town. Boat rides can take you into the wetlands of the Mompox Depression which spread out to the horizon, giving a home to giant iguanas and tropical birds. Mompox is a natural stopping point while making your way from the Caribbean coast of Cartagena back into the mountain ranges of central Colombia. The road from Cartagena to Mompox is paved but the ride can be long and hot. Lasting around 7 hours the road cuts straight through arid terrain composed of low lying scrub brush and sparse trees.

DAY 9 — Mompox to Bucaramanga - 350KM / 217MI

Bucaramanga is the capital of the Santander Department, a huge sprawling city set on the foothills of the magnificent Eastern Andes Mountains. The historic center is amazing, with whitewashed chapels and the towering Sagrada Familia Cathedral. There's a fun water park (Acualago) and wonderful botanical gardens if you have time to explore after your long ride day. The main reason to visit Bucaramanga is because it's a natural stopping point en route to San Gil, Baricharra, Chicamocha Canyon, and the general area of exploring the department of Santander.

↑ Mompox is a town frozen in time and looks as it used to be during colonial times in the 1500's

DAY 9 — Bucaramanga to San Gil & Barichara - 98KM / 61MI

A shorter ride day today, southbound, will see you at San Gil and Baricharra, considered Colombia's capitals of adventure sports. You can literally spend a week up here whitewater rafting, paragliding, horseback riding, hiking, caving, rappelling, and more. As usual, getting there is half the fun and this route is no different, taking you through the famous Chicamocha Canyon.

LARGER THAN THE GRAND CANYON - Have you ever wished that you can ride to the bottom of the Grand Canyon? Larger than the Grand Canyon, Chicamocha Canyon is covered with roads and switchbacks which make it possible to ride your motorcycle to the bottom, cross the river then ride back up the other side. Chicamocha Canyon drops down 2,000m (6,560ft) at its deepest point. The terrain is arid semi-desert and speckled with cactus so be sure to bring extra water and wear your sunscreen. Riding through endless switchback curves the journey ends at the well preserved colonial town of Barichara or the adventure sports town of San Gil.

SAN GIL VS. BARICHARA - San Gil is where all the river-based action plays out: this is a much bigger working town that offers a ton of exciting excursions (like the whitewater rafting, bungee jumping kayaking, paragliding, etc) and a much livelier evening scene. Baricharra, on the other hand, is a more charming but smaller and quieter village but this is the best base for amazing hikes. Barricharra is an enchanting town, one that's often used as a movie set for Colombian telenovelas.

OUR PICK WOULD BE TO HEAD TO BARICHarra early in the day, park up, look around, and be in San Gil by the afternoon, to plan whatever crazy adrenaline-pumping sport you like best for the next day. If you're an extreme-sport junky, this is the kind of area that's likely to kidnap you for an entire week! (Although most people just spend a couple of days)

OPTIONAL ROUTE -

EL COCUY NATIONAL PARK - 234km / 145mi

Absolutely mindblowing! One of the best and least-explored wilderness areas of Colombia, El Cocuy National Park is all about sapphire-hued lakes, snow-drenched high peaks, and spectacular ancient glaciers which are fast disappearing. Over the last five decades, more than half of Colombia's glaciers have melted so if there's ever been a time to visit this region on two wheels, now is it. You can ride into the park, all the way to the start of the hiking trail to Ritacuba, by far the most accessible glacier in this region. The town of El Cocuy is the best base to explore the park but the entrance is still an hour's ride away – spend the night here, ride up in the morning and spend a full day hiking the somewhat limited but still sensational trails.

JEFF & ALAN'S GUIDE TO MOTORCYCLE TRAVEL IN COLOMBIA

DAY 10

San Gil to Barbosa
- 193km / 120mi

Quebrada Las Gachas, Santander - Quebrada Las Gachas is a series of natural "jacuzzi-like" pools along a shallow river bed. Covered in colorful algae the river has been called Santander's Cano Cristales. There is a 10 to 15-minute walk to get there, but it's worth the effort and the views are gorgeous.

OPTIONAL TRIP: WINDOWS OF TISQUIZOQUE - This hidden-secret is straight out of Jurassic Park. We love visiting here on our tours and although we'd love it to remain secret, we'd be amiss if we didn't include it here. Tisiquizoque is a spectacular three-tiered waterfall that emerges from a cave set high up on the side of a mountain (the window) and cascades down 300 jaw-dropping meters of freefall. Best part? You can actually hike up into the mountain where the fall originates and follow the path of the river until the moment it plummets. There is also another trail that takes you to the bottom of the waterfall which is equally cool but without the huge panoramic view

DAY 11

Barbosa to Medellín
- 367km / 228mi

Either one full day of riding or 2 will see you back home taking you through the towns of Landázuri, Cimitarra, and Puerto Berrio before arriving in Medellín

↑ Medellín is truly a cosmopolitan city with a million things to do.

144 ColombiaMotoAdventures.com

① Chicamocha Canyon is covered with roads and switchbacks which make it possible to ride your motorcycle to the bottom, cross the river then ride back up

Exploring The Eastern Mountain Ranges

This 16-day trip explores Colombia's Eastern Ranges (Cordillera Oriental), widely regarded as the most rugged of the country's three Andean ranges. Lesser-known, lesser-visited, and with an insane array of exhilarating roads that are tailor-made for motorcycle touring, the Eastern Ranges are home to some of our favorite motorcycle-playgrounds.

THERE'S SOMETHING HERE FOR EVERYONE – Short ride days leave us plenty of time to enjoy the more cultural and historic destinations whilst longer riding days, on winding mountain roads, place the emphasis on the riding experience and the sensational landscapes. This itinerary has something for everyone: fast riding on paved roads, rough roads to get the juices flowing, high-altitude passes, and spectacular low-lying valleys.

THE WILD, WILD EAST – Ride your motorcycle from Medellín straight east to the Cordillera Oriental, home to some of the most exciting motorbiking routes in the country

CLIMB THE ROCK - Soak up "the most spectacular views in Colombia" from the top of famous Piedra del Peñol in Guatapé, with its 740-step stairway to the heavens

PÁRAMO - Fantastic high-altitude riding across the Colombian Páramo, one of the world's rarest and most biodiverse ecosystems – enjoy the country's longest road ascent!

ANTIOQUIA – Colombia's second-biggest agricultural powerhouse, the Antioquia region is primarily mountainous although it's dotted with an array of verdant valleys – sensational landscapes that make for rewarding motorcycle riding

BOCAYÁ – Right at the heart of Colombia's fight for independence, the Department of Bocaya flanks the Easter Mountains and is renowned for its exquisite towns, an abundance of wilderness, dramatic peaks, and densely forested valley – a biker's absolute dream ride

JAW-DROPPING ROADS & SCENERY– Enjoy the kind of sensory overload that can only be experienced when riding a motorcycle through a kaleidoscope of landscapes, altitudes, and climates

DAY 1 — Medellín to Guatapé
(99km / 62mi)

Guatapé really does make for a sensational first-stop out of Medellín. Whatever you do, don't miss it! An interesting fact is that the rock in Guatapé, called la Piedra del Peñol in Spanish) is technically an inselberg, which literally translates to 'island mountain' from the original German. This is a type of rock formation that rises abruptly from gently sloping or virtually level surrounding plains. The largest inselberg in the world is Uluru, in Australia - yet that, as opposed to Guatapé, can no longer be climbed as of 2019.

 Recommended Hotel: **Zocalo Campestre**

After coming down from the mighty rock, you can find a comfy spot at a nearby restaurant with a view of the lake. Order a huge bandeja paisa complete with beans, rice, chorizo and avocado, and of course, a cold beer or guanabana juice.

And don't listen to anyone that tells you this is a tourist trap: some tourist attractions are just too good to ignore!

DAY 2
Guatapé to Sonsón
(140km / 87mi)

This is going to be an interesting trip. Today we ride to the former guerilla conflict zone of Sonsón. Sonsón has been off-limits for decades due to guerilla activity. Although it's safe now there is very little information on the internet about the area. Consequently, it's untouched by tourism which makes it the perfect place to get an authentic taste of Colombia.

The ride to Sonsón is great. One of the best things about this ride is the miles and miles of exciting twists and turns. Ups, downs, ascending curves, descending curves, increasing radius curves, decreasing radius curves. You're going to get a ton of riding experience on just this one road. The pavement here is in good shape and as is the case in lots of areas in the countryside, there is very little traffic.

Midway we're going to stop off at Luisa's house and have a cup of local

 Recommended Hotel:
El Tesoro

coffee called tinto. If you like kids you'll be delighted to meet her twin toddlers. Tourists never stop here and you'll see how happy she is to talk with us. Besides being a fun way to connect with the locals, it's a way to directly support a family business.

We'll visit the HALO demining operations and learn about their efforts to remove leftover anti-personnel landmines from the area. We get the chance to hold deactivated landmines they have recovered. Yep, there are still landmines out here.

The town of Sonsón is located at a high elevation but we're going to climb even higher. The Páramo de Sonsón is a lookout point that stands at over 10,000ft in elevation. The lookout has a scenic view of the fog rolling across the cloud forest and nearby valley. By now it will be late afternoon and we'll head back to town to check in to our hotel and grab a pizza and a beer.

We stay at the El Tesoro hotel located on the main square. This is a 200-year-old mansion that has been converted into a unique hotel. Unlike other hotels, this one hasn't been updated and still retains its original charm. In addition, the hotel is somewhat of a museum and is filled with an eclectic collection of antiques. Looking over everything will keep you captivated for hours.

Located next door to the hotel is a great pizza restaurant. From the second-story balcony, we can enjoy a brick oven pizza while people-watching on the main square. Sonsón leaves the warm weather of Guatapé behind. Located at 8,100ft you'll want to bring a jacket because it's going to be cold at night.

↑ Main square in Sonsón

DAY 3 — Sonsón to Salamina (87km / 54mi)

Salamina is Colombia's best-kept secret. Tucked away in a far off corner of the coffee region, the beauty of Salamina is a sight to behold. The town itself is situated on the peak of a mountain, with entire streets sometimes appearing as if they are about to slide off the side of the mountain. Once we enter the town, we see why it has earned national heritage status. Houses climb the sloping streets with each one determined to outdo its neighbors. Elaborate woodworking takes the form of intricately decorated doors, windows, balconies, and zócalos (the distinct lower sections of the whitewashed facades). It's hard to walk the streets of Salamina without constantly looking upward at the flower-filled balconies. A gorgeous bronze basin fountain made in Paris sits in the central plaza surrounded by tall trees and benches. In 1900 the fountain was brought to town on the back of ox and mules and since then it has become a symbol of the region. There are also various restaurants surrounding the main square where you can try typical local dishes, including the local favorite of steamed eggs (Huevos al Vapor), which is made with the help of an espresso machine.

The road from Sonsón is unpaved but in good condition. Almost as soon as we leave Sonsón we have to stop to take photos of the expansive valley right outside of town. The rest of the ride consists of windy roads and spectacular views of the surrounding coffee and sugarcane plantations. In the middle of the trip, we drop into a warm valley and cross a bridge over a white water river before snaking back into the mountains on the other side. Just before we arrive in town, there's a panoramic view of the town precariously sitting on the top of a hill.

 Recommended Hotel: **Casa de Lola Garcia**

One of the nicer boutique options in Salamina is the Casa de Lola Garcia. Formerly a coffee hacienda, the owners have beautifully restored the house and converted it into a charming boutique hotel. The property is complete with spacious rooms, king-sized beds, and a beautiful courtyard with jasmine trees and a jacuzzi. The hotel has a perfect location and is only a two-minute walk from the main square.

DAY 4 — Free Day in Salamina (87km / 54mi)

 Recommended Hotel: **Casa de Lola Garcia**

When you have these many days at your disposal, you certainly don't want to miss that side trip to the Samaria Valley, which you can easily take from Salamina. Valley, which you can easily take from Salamina.

DAY 5 — Salamina to Mariquita (188km / 117mi)

 Recommended Hotel: **Casa de Lola Garcia**

The sensory overload of this wicked trip continues today as you take to the road for the long but beautiful ride to Mariquita, a town drenched in historic ruins and sensational natural surroundings that hide a bevy of waterfalls. We leave the high-altitude mountains behind to soak up the heat of the low-lying valleys.

DAY 6 — Mariquita to Bogotá (175km / 109mi)

Today we tackle a 2,200m (7,200ft) ascent to reach Bogotá, the capital of Colombia. You'll need steely nerves to tackle traffic in the big city BUT you'll be rewarded with a steaming bowl of ajiaco soup, a Bogotá specialty that packs an insanely tasty punch.

JEFF & ALAN'S GUIDE TO MOTORCYCLE TRAVEL IN COLOMBIA

DAY 7 — Bogotá to Tauramena
(305km / 190mi)

Dodging the morning peak-hour traffic out of Bogotá will be our main priority today, and you'll be mightily glad for the early start given this will be our longest riding day of the whole trip. Settle you rear-end into that saddle, polish that visor and settle in for a phenomenal ride.

The blink-and-you'll-miss-it town of Tauramena is your aim today but you'll be passing several charming towns along the way that make for excellent leg-stretching breaks so we'll take it easy and really soak up the scenery.

The region of Causanare is not usually on many tourist's wish-lists but we think this is one of Colombia's hidden gems: luscious plains home to wildlife, a fantastic array of dramatic landscapes along the foothills of the Eastern Andes and, if truth be told, some of the best coffee in all of Colombia.

Today is about wilderness, winding roads, and wonderful sights!

DAY 8 — Tauramena to Socha
(210km / 130mi)

Back up to the high-altitude Andes you ride today as you aim for Socha (2,700masl / 8,757ft), the gateway to the spectacular snowy peaks of El Cocuy. This region holds a special place in the heart of all Colombians, as this was the site of the famous Battle of Bocoya' in 1819, the final push that drove the Spaniards out and secured independence for New Granada, modern-day Colombia.

This land of eye-popping vistas is revered for its incredible nature and welcoming people and is considered one of the best hiking destinations in the country, that's way off the beaten path.

This is a side of Colombia not many even know exists, let alone visit.

Cocuy National Park has glaciated peaks reaching over 17,000 feet and tons of rarely explored alpine terrain.

JEFF & ALAN'S GUIDE TO MOTORCYCLE TRAVEL IN COLOMBIA

↑ A typical Colombian cowboy.

DAY 10
El Cocuy to Soatá
(88km / 55mi)

After a spectacular sunrise over the Sierra Nevada of El Cocuy, hop on your saddle and head back down the western slopes of the Andes to Soatá (1,950 masl /6,397ft), a charming town framed by forested hills that are home to some of Colombia's rarest and most endangered birds.

Soatá boasts an interesting history that dates back over 550 years. Nowadays, locals still lead a predominantly subsistence-farming life and you'll find the surroundings dotted with ranches and farms. The cultivation of dates is a huge business here and the town is considered the date palm capital of Colombia.

DAY 11
Soatá to San Gil
(145km / 90mi)

If you're a lover of extreme sports, then San Gil is the one town on this itinerary that you may have heard about. If you prefer to get your thrills on a bike instead, enjoy the magnificent ride to San Gil and, once there, head up to El Penon Guane viewpoint and restaurant, where you can sip a cold cerveza and soak up the resplendent views. The town is a gem of wonderful colonial-era architecture, brimming with steep roads and friendly locals – somehow, the extreme sport tourism has left its laid-back mark on San Gil, making it a very enjoyable place to spend the night.

DAY 9
Socha to El Cocuy
(113km / 70mi)

The New York Times named El Cocuy 'The Secret Colombia Above the Clouds" and it's indeed true that, at this breath-taking altitude, you'll experience the country from a whole new perspective. On the bikes, it'll feel as if we're tickling the skies, riding dizzying altitudes (almost 5,000masl/16,404ft!), and being totally overwhelmed by the snow-capped peaks that surround us on all sides. The El Cocuy National Park may be unknown outside dedicated hiking circles but, for those in the know, the peaks here represent Colombia's last true untamed wilderness. Crazy guys with ropes and crampons (and antifreeze in their veins) head here to tackle unbelievable trails, cross ancient glaciers and skirt iridescent lakes of a thousand shades of blue.

ColombiaMotoAdventures.com

DAY 12 — Free Day in San Gil (220km / 136mi) - White Water Rafting

San Gil straddles the Rio Fonce (a very popular whitewater rafting destination) and is strategically located near some of the country's most impressive canyons (like Chichamocha) where adrenalin-addicts get their canyoning, bungee-jumping, extreme kayaking, rafting, and paragliding fix. Use today to enjoy some extreme sports or just chill out and enjoy the town.

DAY 13 — San Gil to Duitama (220km / 136mi)

Lining the shores of the Chicamocha River at an altitude of 2,522masl (8,274ft), Duitama is yet another adventure-sport and cultural gem of the Cordillera Oriental. Right nearby is where you'll find Pueblito Boyacense, a kind of 'condensed' representation of the Boyaca Department's eclectic mix of architecture, customs, and cultures. This all-in-one village reproduction may sound like a kitschy tourist-trap but is, in fact, a fascinating and immensely relaxing place to visit – even though you may by now have seen enough Eastern Mountain towns to get the gist of the fusion of cultures here. Duitama is a charming mountain town, famous for being a pit-stop on the Tour Colombia professional cycling race, so you know those ascents and hairpin turns are gonna be epic! The town's colonial core is home to a gorgeous cathedral and a vibrant main plaza (Plaza de Los Libertadores) that's a hive of social activity, especially on sunny weekends.

DAY 14: Duitama to Villa de Leyva
(92 km / 57 mi)

The colonial village of Villa de Leyva is revered for boasting the biggest cobblestone plaza in the whole continent and, although the square is impressive enough, the town's authentic vibe is the real highlight. Given its proximity to Bogotá, Villa de Leyva is one of the most touristy towns in this region but, trust us, it remains an unmissable destination on your tour.

Casa Terracota - The coolest place to visit in Villa de Leyva is definitely the Casa Terracota. Only a 10minute ride from the main square, This unique house looks like it's out of a Dr. Seuss book and is made out of nothing else but clay. We recommend spending an hour exploring the maze of rooms. Please be careful when you arrive there as we have heard they blocked the entrance with a barely visible cord.

↑ The cobbled stone plaza of Villa de Leyva

↑ Located in Villa de Leyva, the Casa Terracota is basically a giant piece of pottery

DAY 15: Villa de Leyva to Otanche
(136km / 84mi)

Often dubbed "The Forgotten Paradise", the area around small and unassuming Otanche is an expansive region of dense forests that hides a stunning cache of natural wonders. This is a land of hidden canyons dotted with multi-tiered waterfalls, emerald-hued lakes and rivers, and an abundance of caves inhabited by an array of colorful, exotic birds. The ride down towards the Magdalena Valley, and Otanche, is extraordinary.

Eastern Carib tribes were the first to settle in this area (and also the first to mine for emeralds) but they were almost totally wiped out by the Spanish in the late 16th century. Nowadays, the area around Otanche is recognized for its prime biodiversity and much of it is set aside as a protected reserve.

DAY 16: Otanche to Medellín
(300KM / 186MI)

This morning, after an early breakfast, you can set off on the long ride home, soaking up the last of the superlative scenery. It's time to bring this unforgettable adventure to an end.

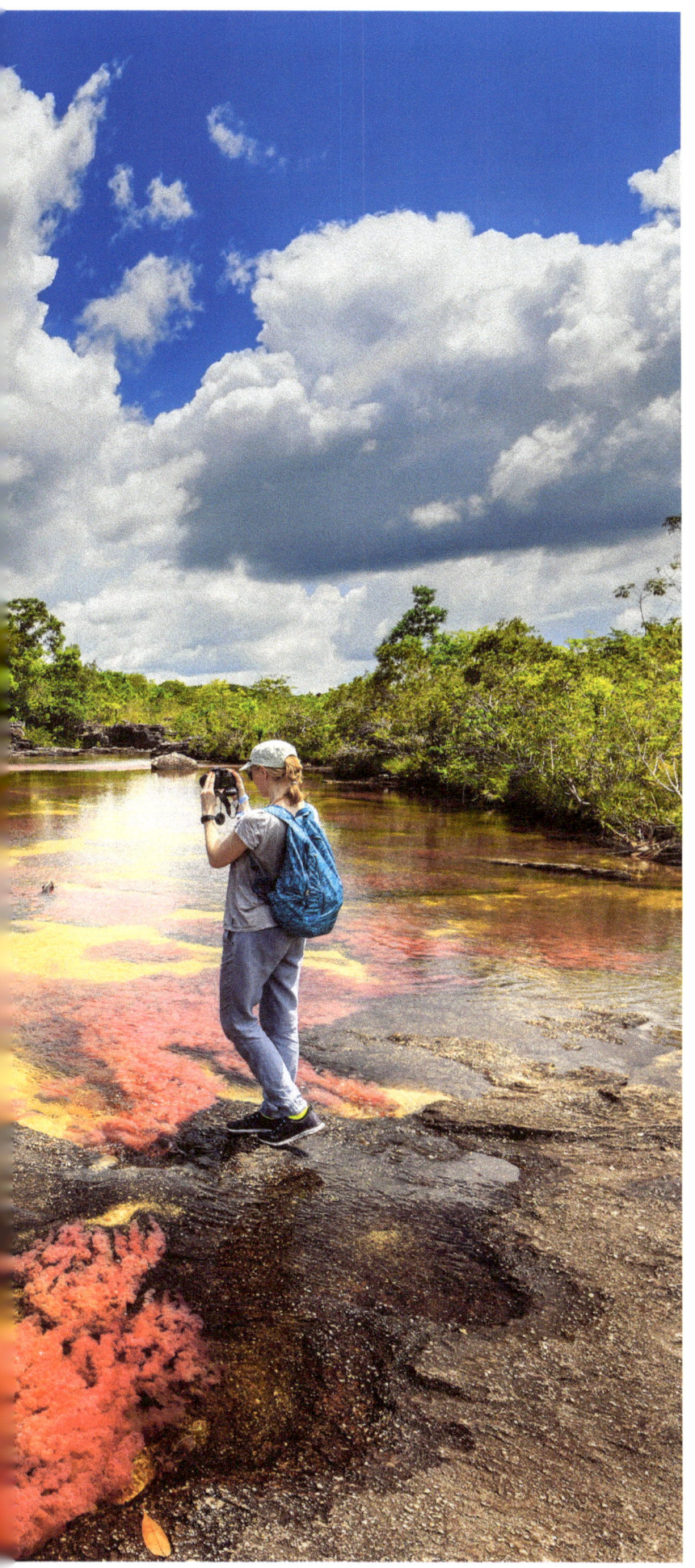

CAÑO CRISTALES

Uniquely rare in rivers of the world, the waters of Caño Cristales appear to be a liquid rainbow. For several months every year, the water appears to turn into vivid hues of red, yellow, blue, green, and even black. Being an extremely unique phenomena, this color change is actually due to the mass-blooming of an endemic plant species called Macarenia clavígera. This flowering water plant is incredibly rare, growing only in a few tropical climates of the world. Caño Cristales is the only place where it blooms so prolifically and spectacularly. Unfortunately, the colors can only be seen at a certain time of year, from mid-May to early December.

The route to Caño Cristales is hardcore. If you like river crossings, sand, rocks, and mud this is the trip for you. Warning: This route is extremely remote, and at certain times of the year, impassable, due to deep mud. We recommend having an adventure prepped bike complete with knobby tires as well as bringing ropes to help pull you out of the mud in case you get stuck.

Where Not To Go

THE WORST ROAD IN COLOMBIA

Colombia is filled with fantastic riding, but there are some places that you should stay away from, and El Alto de la Línea is one of them. El Alto de la Línea (The Line) is a mountain pass that cuts through the daunting Cordillera Central mountain range stretching from Armenia to Ibague. Due to lack of railroads, the main form of transporting goods in Colombia is by truck, and the road serves a vital artery for truck traffic transporting goods from the Pacific port city of Buenaventura to Bogotá. Road builders had to find a way to cross, and since they weren't able to build around or tunnel through, they were forced to go up and over. What resulted was a road that is anything but linear.

Twisting its way through the landscape at a maximum altitude of 3.287m (10,787ft), The Line is littered with heavy truck-traffic, copious rain and fog, making it one of the most chaotic and hair-raising passes in all of South America. Overloaded tractor-trailers and slow-moving buses try to huff and puff their way to the top. Frequent traffic jams occur due to serious accidents or broken-down vehicles with overheated engines.

Passing in traffic like this is extremely difficult, and you won't find many places to do it safely. Locals try to earn money by acting as human traffic signals by standing on blind curves waving flags, warning drivers of traffic coming the opposite way. One mistake in the low visibility or wet pavement can lead to you being squished by a truck or falling off the edge of a cliff into the valley below.

Coming down the pass isn't any easier, with low visibility making it nearly impossible to be seen by oncoming traffic. Even worse, there is no place to stop, so the air becomes filled with the acrid stench of burning brake pads. A notable lack of escape lanes makes any truck driver whose brakes fail find out the hard way that the only emergency exit is by either smashing into the side of a rock wall or falling over a cliff. All those factors combined make La Linea have an accident rate four times higher than the national average.

Expect traffic jams and heavy truck traffic on the Alto de La Linea

↑ Bogotá ranked #1 as the most congested city in the world.

> Bogotá's population is comparable to that of New York City but with only half the area. This population density helps create the traffic nightmare called Bogotá.

There is some good news, though: After a decade of work Colombia has finally opened the longest tunnel in South America, called the "Túnel de la Línea." At a length of 8.65 km (5.4 miles) and a cost of $270 million US dollars, the tunnel bypasses the mountain's peak and provides an easier link to the cities of Calarcá, Quindío, and Cajamarca, Tolima. This will save up to 80 minutes of travel time for some vehicles as well as increase the average speed of the pass from 18.2 kilometers per hour (11.3 mph) to 60 kilometers per hour (37 mph).

Still want to give it a try? We recommend you do as the locals do and say a prayer before attempting the road.

BOGOTÁ

Bogotá's traffic is bad. In fact, it's the worst. A 2019 global traffic survey Bogotá ranked #1 as the most congested city in the world. Bogotá's population is comparable to that of New York City but with only half the area. This population density helps create a traffic nightmare called Bogotá. In fact, the average urban speed in Bogotá is only 9mph.

Just how bad is traffic? Years ago the Mayor of Bogotá famously hired 420 mimes to make fun of traffic violators.

Besides soul-crushing traffic, Bogotá has crime. But I thought that you said that Colombia is safe? Colombia is safe, but Bogotá has crime. In fact, Bogotá is a cesspool of crime, from muggings to identity fraud to plain, old rip-off artists. This has led to a pretty depressing overall climate. This is a city where no one trusts one another or tries to help one another very much.

Bogotá is also cold and polluted. The moral of the story is, stay out of Bogotá if you can.

SALENTO

There's a saying that says "Pijao is the new Filandia, Filandia is the new Salento, and Salento now doesn't exist." You may feel compelled to go to Salento since every single guide book ever written about Colombia

↑ Valle del Cocora, Colombia - Willy Jeeps waiting to take tourists back to Salento

talks about. Salento is a charming town around 6 hours from Medellín. The town's center is chock-full of local craft shops and vibrant colonial architecture painted in rainbow hues. Salento is also close to the famous Valle Cocora where you can explore a valley full of towering wax-palm trees. So what's not to like? Crowds of people.

Salento and the Valle Cocora have become filled with mobs of people and have basically lost their charm. Crowds of tourists from all over have overrun Salento because thinking that it's still the quaint village that it once was and that they can see the "real Colombia" in Salento. This has led to a boom in construction, traffic, cheap restaurants, and backpacker hostels. It's now basically a plastic Disney World version of Colombia where you can buy an overpriced cupcake to an overpriced T-shirt. It's also filled with locals lining the streets offering everything from being your guide for a few hours to rip-off 2 hour-long horseback rides that only go about a kilometer into the valley. Salento used to be cool but it isn't anymore. If you're looking for authentic towns to visit there are tons of them besides Salento.

A couple of great alternatives to Salento are Filandia and Pijao. Located nearby, Filandia can be thought of as the less touristic brother of Salento. It's a great option if you want to experience a Coffee Region town without the crowds. We

> Salento and the Valle Cocora have become filled with mobs of people and have basically lost their charm. Crowds of tourists from all over have overrun Salento thinking that it's still the quaint village that it once was and that they can see the "real Colombia"

recommend checking out "La Colina Iluminada." This wooden lookout tower is over 18 meters (60 feet) tall and offers breathtaking panoramic views over three different Colombian departments: Quindio, Risaralda, and Valle del Cauca. On a clear morning, it's even possible to spot the distant snow-capped peaks of Los Nevados National Park. Afterward, you can grab a bite to eat at Helena Adentro, one of the best restaurants in the region. The restaurant is picturesque, and the food is excellent serving Colombian-inspired main courses as well as typical tapas-style dishes with a twist.

The second option is the isolated village of Pijao. Tucked away in the Andes, Pijao is accessed via a narrow, winding mountain road that takes you by lush forests, coffee plantations, and farms growing plantains. Be sure to stop and grab a coffee at the Mirador Cafe Concorde restaurant on the way.

Once you arrive at Pijao you will find that it is a lovely quiet town with very friendly people and lots of little cafes and town bars. The main square is decorated with flowers and has beautiful views of the mountains. Coffee tours here are popular as well as visits to some of the waterfalls located nearby.

Pijao is laid back and has kept its cultural heritage and architecture of colonial centuries. This has earned it the distinction of being designated as the first "Slow City" in Latin America. This means that the town focuses on improving its quality of life by reducing stress and slowing down its overall pace. If you're looking for a relaxed, authentic, and off-the-beaten-track place to visit, we highly recommend Pijao.

Jeff Cremer Interview

What's your background?
I'm originally from Pueblo, Colorado in the United States.

How did you get to Colombia?
After university, I decided to backpack through Central America. I eventually settled down and lived in Peru for over thirteen years, although I have worked all over Latin America during that time. A friend invited me to visit her in Colombia. After so many years of living in Peru, I thought that it was time for a change, so I took her up on the offer and moved to Colombia. I felt that the people were the friendliest strangers that I ever met, and the landscapes were beautiful.

How/why did you get into the motorcycle business?
Getting involved in the motorcycle world was a complete accident. My parents always told me that motorcycles were dangerous. I never really considered riding on a motorcycle until I had the chance to go for a ride with one of my friends in Cali, Colombia. Even though I was a passenger, From the second that I got on, I was hooked. My friend told me, "Amigo, you need to get a motorcycle" I said, "but I don't know how to ride one", He said, "Learn." So my Colombian friend, Orlando, taught me how to ride a motorcycle, and I've been riding ever since.

My first motorcycle was a little red Honda CBR 125. I loved that bike and drove all over Colombia with it. Even though the bike was small and relatively slow, it still got the job done, and I was able to see a lot of the country. I actually think it's one of the reasons that I love Colombia so much. While I was visiting the United States, I had the chance to purchase a BMW G650GS. I toured throughout the mountains of Colorado and the desert southwest with it. I had so much fun touring around on motorcycles that I decided to turn my passion into a business. Now my business is exactly that. Sharing my passion for motorcycles and traveling

> *The thing I like most about the tours, besides seeing exciting stuff, is being able to make friends and talk to fascinating people.*

around Colombia with people from all over the world.

Is Colombia Safe?
Security isn't an issue here. I lived in Cali, Colombia, in 2009 before recently moving back. I have been all over the country and have never felt unsafe or threatened. If anything, the people are overly friendly and always wanting to come over to say hi and help you with anything you need. As they say in Colombia: The only risk in Colombia is wanting to stay.

What's the best thing about leading tours? I've heard some tour guides say it's like a cattle drive. What has been your experience?
I led expeditions in the Peruvian Amazon for years with small groups of people and scientists. The people who go on these types of tours are fascinating. They are usually smart, adventurous people who enjoy getting out of their comfort zone and seeing some amazing once in a lifetime things. The thing that I like most about the tours, besides seeing exciting stuff, is being able to become friends with and talk to fascinating people. I've met people from Canada's top neurosurgeon to a former translator for the president of Ethiopia. I've never really had the experience of babysitting a bus full of "sheeple."

Worst thing about leading tours?
The end. Sometimes it's kinda sad when the tour ends, and everyone has to go their separate ways after having an awesome time touring around.

Do you have any funny stories/anecdotes from any tours?
I was returning to Medellín with a client after spending the day exploring the mountains. We were on a road when some people waved us down and said that the road ahead was closed due to a mudslide. We were looking at the map and talking about taking a longer route back when some locals offered to take us around the landslide. It turned out to be a fantastic adventure consisting of a nighttime ride on an abandoned railway that was converted to a remote jungle path. The trail took through three or four train tunnels as well as passing cows sleeping on the road. We also made a random stop for the lady to pick up wood shavings for her chickens.

All of a sudden, all the bikes stopped. We were about ready to cross an abandoned train bridge standing about 250ft above a river. The bridge had old wooden boards on the sides of the tracks that we could walk or drive down, but they didn't exactly inspire confidence. There was a tiny section of concrete in the middle of the tracks, and it was just wide enough for me to put my front tire on. I spread out my feet so they would touch the other train tracks on either side of me and cracked open the throttle. I slid my feet down the sides of the rails while slowly guiding the bike across the bridge.

Once we got to the other side we were all giving each other high five's and celebrating the fact that we made it. It's just one of those cool random adventures that pop up when riding around Colombia and make it a special place.

I heard that you used to be a photographer in the Amazon jungle.
I started doing photography as a hobby about 20 years ago. I was interested in astronomy and began taking pictures of nebula and galaxies. After that, I started taking pictures of other things, ants, flowers, etc. and just kept going. I

JEFF & ALAN'S GUIDE TO MOTORCYCLE TRAVEL IN COLOMBIA

owned a website that allowed me to travel all over and do lots of photography. I sold my website to an investor about ten years ago and then sat down and thought about what I was going to do next. I knew that I liked photography and I always had the idea to become a photographer, so I decided to do it. I wound up working in the jungle and getting published in National Geographic, Discovery Channel, Wired Magazine, and tons of other places. My parents are proud of me and love my pictures, and that's better than any amount of money or fame I could ever get. I went back home to visit a few years ago and it was kinda interesting to see some of the first pictures I ever took hanging on the wall in my old room. I never thought that I would accomplish all the stuff that I did.

What's it like to work in the Peruvian Amazon? What are some of your most memorable "wow" moments photographing wildlife?
Ufff..There have been so many interesting things that I've seen: jaguars, harpy eagles, gigantic snakes, and even spent time seeking out uncontacted tribes. During my time in the jungle, we discovered several new species. We found a predatory glow worm that lives in a mud wall, a spider that draws a picture of itself in its web using leaves, and a tiny spider that used its silk to construct a tower with a picket fence-like structure around it. We also found a minuscule spider that created a slingshot out of silk and used it to fling itself at flying mosquitos. We even found a furry yellow caterpillar that people say looks like Donald Trump's hair!

I have a background in extreme high-resolution photography, so I was able to take some incredible high-resolution images over my career. I took the world's highest resolution image of Machu Picchu, which weighs in at 16 gigapixels. The resolution is insane, and you can zoom into the image and see incredible detail. Some of these images were published in "EARTH - Platinum Edition", the world's largest atlas. Each page spread of this limited edition book measures a breathtaking 6 feet x 9 feet. Only 31 copies were printed, each retailing for $100,000 a copy.

What's your favorite tour?
Without a doubt, I would have to say that it's the Lost Emerald City. I love adventure and seeking out unique and unusual places. I had heard that many emeralds came from Colombia, so I decided to take a trip off the beaten path and find out exactly where they came from. Lots of people say, "off the beaten path", but this trip truly takes us to one of the most amazing and unknown destinations of Colombia. It's like something from medieval times.

Formerly the most dangerous place in the world the region was sealed off from the outside world for decades due to intense fighting. The area is now open for the first time in decades after a peace treaty with the guerilla groups was signed.

Now the area is a peaceful and beautiful place. We can put on boots and work side by side with artisanal emerald miners known as "guaqueros" to search for the precious stones. It's also an excellent opportunity for documentary photography as well as a chance to speak with emerald miners about life in the mining camps and surrounding areas. The trip is truly a once in a lifetime adventure and completely different from any other trip I've ever taken.

JEFF & ALAN'S GUIDE TO MOTORCYCLE TRAVEL IN COLOMBIA

Alan Churchill Interview

What's your background?
Like my friend Jeff, I am from the USA, but as a child, I grew up in former French and British colonies of the Caribbean. Those years created a comfort with other cultures and people of different languages that today drives my love for travel and adventures. I've ridden motorcycles in Vietnam, Costa Rica, and Cuba, but my favorite is Colombia.

How did you get to Colombia?
Like many people, I heard that it was dangerous and never considered going there. However, about ten years ago, I started reading blogs about motorcycle travel through Central and South America. Time after time, reports surfaced that Colombia was different from the rest of the Latin American countries, and the writers wanted to return. One motorcyclist even sold everything back home and opened a hotel in Colombia. People who traveled there weren't writing about the danger but of the friendliness of the people and the beauty of riding. One day at church in the USA, I met a Venezuelan government official who was fleeing political persecution. He connected me to his motorcycle club with members in Colombia. Through the internet, I arranged to rent a couple of motorcycles from a member and his son. After three weeks of riding Colombia, I was hooked.

> After three weeks of riding in Colombia, I was hooked.

How/why did you get involved with motorcycles?
When I was a kid, I was fascinated with anything that had a motor. I took some nighttime auto mechanic courses with adults and the instructor thought that it was so cool that I had an interest that he took me under his wing and became my mentor for all things mechanical. I took courses in foreign car repair and auto paint and body. I enjoyed it so much that it's become a hobby that I still do to this day.

Keeping with the theme of cars and mechanics, I happened to buy a Kymco 150 scooter that required a motorcycle license. I didn't know much about them and was actually scared of motorcycles at the beginning. I still thought that I'd give it a try and signed up for the motorcycle safety course to get my licence. Through the course, I learned that it wasn't as dangerous as I thought it was and that there were many techniques for minimizing risk and riding safely.

The Kymco became a starter for more bikes and through the years and I've had a DR200, Vstrom 650 and Honda Africa Twin.

I would go motorcycle camping with friends in the North Carolina mountains. We would pack our saddle bags and spend the night in the forest. You really have to have everything in order and I enjoy the challenge of planning trips to remote areas as well as finding small and lightweight gear to bring.

As I mentioned, after riding through several other countries, I was hooked on Colombia. I flew back for some more riding, renting from a legitimate motorcycle company with insurance that actually covered me. There I met the owner, Jeff, and after buying a motorcycle of my own, we've traveled a lot of miles on group tours exploring Colombia.

I've had so much fun that sharing the experience in a guide book was something that I just had to do. This country is so big and diverse that I'll be exploring it on motorcycles for years. Who knows, maybe one day we'll cross paths on one of the many beautiful roads in Colombia!

What's your favorite tour?
Honestly, I really like the emerald mining tour, but I also like the Windows of Tisquizoque tour. I saw pictures of a river flowing out of a huge hole in the face of a high cliff, and I was so fascinated about how thousands of gallons of water could be flowing from a cave that I had to see it for myself. I've traveled all over the world and wanted to see something that I've never seen before. I went there to explore, and it was so cool because I was able to follow the river underground, through a cave and to where it came flowing out of the mountain and then dropping 1000 feet. The waterfalls trip is just one of Colombia's many spectacular sights that you won't find anywhere else.

Do you have any advice for people wanting to visit Colombia?
Traveling Colombia is probably unlike any place you've been before. It's not that difficult, and hundreds of motorcyclists have done it before. It's an unforgettable experience with world-class riding. Don't worry about a thing and come on down!

CONCLUSION

You can definitely do this! You've got everything you need to make this happen. You have itineraries and hotel recommendations, you know where to rent a motorcycle, and you know that Colombia is safe and friendly. All that's left to do is buy your plane ticket and come on down and ride! You're going to have a great time here!

A lot of people worry about not speaking Spanish. Not speaking Spanish isn't a problem. I've had lots of guests come down who didn't speak any Spanish at all and they had a great time. You could have an even better time if you learned a little bit of Spanish but it's not mandatory. If you have some extra time, I recommend taking local Spanish classes for a few days before your trip. It's a great way to get settled in and meet people.

Whether you're planning on traveling with a group of friends or heading off on your own, don't think you're traveling alone. You've already got one friend in Colombia. Motorcycling is my passion and my hobby. I've loved exploring Colombia so much I want to share it with everyone. I just want you to have an awesome trip in Colombia. I'm always available to help you with whatever you need and am just a phone call away.

Come on down and enjoy Colombia. The only risk is wanting to stay!

IMAGE CREDITS:

Police Motorcycles:
Fotos593 / Shutterstock.com
Truck on Mountain:
Oscar Garces / Shutterstock.com
Darien Flags:
Oscar Garces / Shutterstock.com

Everything you need to know about motorcycle travel in Colombia all in one place

World-class riding, that's what Colombia is. From riding through towering, snow-covered volcanoes to descending into a 6000ft deep canyon. From off-road trails through misty jungle mountains to exploring arid coastal deserts. Colombia is a land of extremes. You've probably been dreaming about a trip like this but have had some doubts. What you want is a clear mental picture of riding conditions in the country; what you need is accurate information all in one place. This book is going to give you that and the confidence to do it.

For the past three years, I've owned and operated ColombiaMotoAdventures.com a full-service motorcycle rental and tour agency in Medellín, Colombia. Based on my personal experiences, as well as the experiences of hundreds of satisfied customers, I've compiled as much information as possible and put it all into one place. Even better, it's all up to date and with hundreds of pictures. All this information will have you riding like a local in no time.

TOPICS INCLUDE:

- Is Colombia safe?
- The geography of Colombia
- Multi-day itineraries
- Local driving conditions
- How to buy a motorcycle in Colombia
- Renting a motorcycle
- Recommended motorcycles
- How to fill-up on gas
- Crossing the Darien gap
- Day trips from Medellín

Colombia Motorcycle Adventures, Pajarito Robledo Carrera Cra. 102 #68-36, Medellín, Antioquia, Colombia. +57 321 491 7060
Colombia: +57 321 491 7060   United States: +1 786 623 439360

ColombiaMotoAdventures   colombiamotoadv
ColombiaMotoAdventures.com

www.ingramcontent.com/pod-product-compliance
Lightning Source LLC
Chambersburg PA
CBHW060839010526
44108CB00047B/2838